THE CULT
OF THE
MOON GOD

THE CULT
OF THE
MOON GOD

EXPLODING THE MYTHS OF ISLAM AND DISCOVERING THE TRUTHS OF GOD

BRIAN WILSON

WinePressPublishing
Great Books, Defined.

WinePress Publishing (PO Box 428, Enumclaw, WA 98022) functions only as book publisher. As such, the ultimate design, content, editorial accuracy, and views expressed or implied in this work are those of the author

Unless otherwise noted, all Scriptures are taken from the *Holy Bible, New Living Translation*, copyright © 1996, 2004, 2007 by Tyndale House Foundation. Used by permission of Tyndale House Publishers, Inc., Carol Stream, Illinois 60188. All rights reserved.

Scripture references marked KJV are taken from the *King James Version* of the Bible.

Scripture references marked GNT are taken from the *Good News Translation Bible*, Copyright 1966, 1976 by American Bible Society. This translation is known as the Good News Bible (GNB) around the world.

ISBN 13: 978-1-4141-1997-7
ISBN 10: 1-4141-1997-6
Library of Congress Catalog Card Number: 2010942193

ACKNOWLEDGMENTS

AFTER PRESENTING THIS material numerous times in a public venue, I was encouraged by many of the participants to make it available in book form in order to assist a larger number of people in their endeavor to understand this vital subject matter.

I am grateful to many people for their encouragement. I particularly appreciate the assistance that my friend Dr. D. David has extended to me in proofreading this manuscript and helping to bring it to publication.

Marion K. Coyne and Harry Coyne were instrumental in getting me to begin the process a number of years ago.

Along the way, I appreciated the encouragement of other published authors and friends, including Lee Bear, Dallas Track, and Larry Norman (now deceased).

My wife, Bridgette, helped by proofreading each and every word.

Parts of what I present in this book I have never seen analyzed anywhere else. Most of it, however, comes from my examination of the many resources listed at the conclusion of this presentation. I especially commend to you the work of Dr. Charles Missler and Avi Lipkin.

Finally, I would like to extend my thanks to everyone else who helped bring this book to fruition.

CONTENTS

INTRODUCTION

AFTER THE EVENTS of September 11, 2001, many people experienced a heightened interest in the subject of Islam. I was among them. This heightened interest was entirely warranted, as the non-Islamic world is faced with the greatest challenge to its survival in recorded history. This is not an exaggerated statement. I believe you will see the truth of this as you read through the following pages.

The subject matter for this book was not entirely new for me. I had been studying these things for a number of years, and the many acts of Islamic terrorism over that time, culminating in what has come to be known as 9/11, simply led me to accelerate my intellectual investigation. As my interest and study in this area became known, I found myself asked to teach a class on the subject.

The original intent was for me to fill in for Marion K. Coyne, an accomplished author and speaker in her own right, for one week's session. However, as I prepared the material for the class, I realized this could not be accomplished in one session lasting only sixty to ninety minutes. So I expanded the material and ended up with a course that lasted eight weeks.

After teaching the class, I spoke publicly on the subject of Islam more than forty times in the space of the next few years. (Eventually, I lost count.) Now, in the interest of sounding the warning klaxon, I am presenting this material to you in this format in the hope that you will find it helpful. It is my sincere desire that you will take this matter with the seriousness and gravity it deserves. Your very way of life, as well as that of your children and grandchildren, is at stake.

CHAPTER ONE

THE GREAT ISLAMIC CONSPIRACY

EVEN BEFORE THE tragic events of September 11, 2001, brought names such as al-Qaeda and Osama bin Laden to the forefront of American consciousness, many people were becoming increasingly concerned about the growing threat that Islamic extremism posed to our nation. One such individual was Steven Emerson, an American journalist and author who, in collaboration with the FBI, CIA, and State Department, filmed a documentary, *Terrorists Among Us: Jihad in America*, released in 1994. For his trouble in producing this telling film about the tenets of Islam and the clandestine operations of Islamist groups in the United States, Emerson was blacklisted and received numerous death threats (many of which are still in effect). The program itself was suppressed after limited distribution.

After the attacks on the Pentagon and World Trade Center in 2001, the documentary was updated and rereleased to the public. In the opening to the new edition, Len Sherman, a producer and foreign correspondent, tells a fascinating story about a secret meeting that convened near Washington, D.C., in September 2000. As part of this meeting, a number of respected operatives, analysts, academics, and leaders both inside and outside of government were asked to play a "game." The organizers of this game took the collected theories and convictions of the players about potential threats to American national security and fed them into a computer. The computer then created a number of scenarios that the players were asked collectively to overcome. The object of the exercise was to determine what the *single* greatest threat to America's survival was, and then defeat that threat.

However, as Sherman relates, the outcome of the game did not turn out as the planners had expected. Despite the combined knowledge of the participants and their years of experience in dealing with all kinds of crises, they could not come up with a solution to one especially troublesome threat. As the hours went on, the results and scenarios became darker and more ominous. After ten hours, the players realized that no strategy they employed or diplomatic solution they devised could alter the outcome.

The results of the experiment were so shocking and depressing that the members were asked not to reveal them to the public, for fear it would create a general panic among the populace. For the most part, the members kept to this agreement and have not released the details of the findings. However, we do know that what they determined to be the greatest threat to America's existence did not come from China, an emerging superpower, or Russia, a former superpower, or any single government or state. Instead, the threat came from a *theology*. It came from the ideology of Islamic fundamentalism and, more specifically, the spread of *jihad*, or holy war. As we shall see, America is not the only nation being affected by this ideology. Islamic fundamentalism is spreading throughout Asia, Europe, and Africa as well as in the United States. If this tide is not stemmed, the results will be catastrophic—and all of this will occur within our lifetime.[1]

As frightening as it sounds, this book is about more than just the physical dangers posed by various groups within the Islamic movement. In this study, I hope to show you the truth about Islam and how its practitioners' claims that it is a doctrine of love and peace are false. I want to show you how the tenets of Islam are being subtly imbued into our nation's education system and culture at large. I also hope to dispel the myths that the God of Islam and the God of the Bible are the same and that there is any divine Word of God other than the Bible. Finally, my goal is to compel you to recognize the threat of Islam, understand the truth of what those who practice Islam actually believe, and then compare those beliefs to what we find in the Judeo-Christian Scriptures.

JIHAD AND THE MUSLIM VIEW OF THE AFTERLIFE

Before we continue, it might be good to explain the concept of *jihad* and what those men who choose to die as martyrs in the cause of their religion believe they will obtain in the afterlife. The term *jihad* translates into English as "struggle," and it is used in the Koran to describe "striving in the way of Allah." *Jihad* is an important duty for Muslims and refers to three types of struggles: (1) an internal struggle to maintain faith, (2) the struggle to improve Muslim society, and (3) the struggle of a holy war. These holy wars may be waged against unbelievers, apostates, rebels, and those who do not believe the authority of Islam.[2]

As we will examine later in more detail, this group comprises a significantly large number of people. In fact, there are really only two groups of people in the Islamic universe: the Dar Al Islam, which are those who are faithful to Islam; and the Dar Al Harb, which are those who are not faithful to Islam. Those in the Dar Al Islam are referred to as members of the House of Peace, while those in the Dar Al Harb are called members of the House of War. If you are not a member of the Dar Al Islam—a Muslim believer—then you are a member of the Dar Al Harb, and those who practice Islam are at war with you. Furthermore, they will be at war with you until Judgment Day, for this holy war will only end when the House of Peace conquers the House of War by either converting its members to Islam or killing them.

Islam teaches that those men who die as martyrs in the cause of their religion will receive a reward in the afterlife: "Let those fight in the way of Allah who sell the life of this world for the other. Whoso fighteth in the way of Allah, be he slain or be he victorious, on him we shall bestow a vast reward" (Sura 4:74).

What is this reward? According to the Koran, it is a special place flowing with rivers of wine, where the martyrs receive seven mansions filled with seven virgins waiting to have endless intimacies with them (Sura 47:15; 55:56, 70; 61:10-12). If you do the math, this means that each man will have forty-nine virgins (7 x 7 = 49), although in some areas of the Muslim world you may also hear that these martyrs receive *seventy-two virgins* in one mansion. While there is some disagreement on how this fantasy happens, Muslims do agree on one point: the men who die as martyrs for Allah will get as many virgins to use in the afterlife as they wish.

It was Yasser Arafat (1929–2004), former chairman of the Palestine Liberation Organization (PLO) and founder of the Fatah movement, who was the first to claim that suicide-bombing attacks, where the bomber blew himself up along with innocent people, qualified for this special treatment. Arafat, as we will see, had an interesting career. In the 1990s, after leading his terrorist organizations for a number of years, he met with then-Israeli Prime Minister Yitzhak Rabin and President Bill Clinton in a series of secret talks and negotiations that led to the 1993 Oslo Accords. Out of those meetings, an agreement was reached by which Israel officially recognized the PLO and the PLO officially recognized the state of Israel. The following year, both Arafat and Rabin were awarded the Nobel Peace Prize.

However, at the time security officials had doubts about Arafat's motives, claiming he had "praised suicide bombers as martyrs" and repeatedly "called for a *jihad* (holy war) to liberate Jerusalem." They noted that "Arafat, the veteran terrorist, has created an environment in which terrorists flourish."[3] Based on Arafat's history with the PLO and Fatah movement, these concerns were well founded.

ATROCITIES COMMITTED BY ARAFAT'S REGIME

As ridiculous as it sounds, millions of poor, uneducated Muslims believe the lie that by partaking in suicide bombings they are engaging in a holy war and will receive all of those virgins in paradise for their participation. What is even more surprising is that millions of *educated* Muslims also adhere to this view. These beliefs are among the greatest deceptions of Islam that I hope to dispel. If you don't find them so ridiculous as to be a laughing matter, then they will likely become that way as you read through this book.

What is *not* a laughing matter are the atrocities that Yasser Arafat has committed in the name of Islam. When Arafat met with President Clinton and Hillary Rodham Clinton on the White House lawn in 1993, it represented the first time a sitting president had met with the Palestinian leader or allowed him into the country since Arafat had delivered a speech at the United Nations in 1974. (The Clintons' meeting happened in America at a time when character and politics were clearly chasms apart.) Before this grand reception by the Clintons and his subsequent award of the Nobel Peace Prize, Arafat, acting as a great Islamic leader, had given many orders we would find appalling.

In one instance, Arafat had the bellies of pregnant Arab women split open in front of their husbands. The Palestinian leader gave orders to have Muslim couples who were expecting a child and whom he believed were not faithful enough to radical Islam brought before him. Arafat ordered his followers to hold down the woman while others in his group held down the husband. Then, as the husband was forced to watch, Arafat's men removed the woman's clothing and slit open her belly. Imagine the horror of this moment as the woman screamed and writhed in agony while her husband had to watch in helpless rage. The women victims of this practice most often died.[4]

In performing this practice, Arafat hoped that it would serve as a lesson to less-committed Muslims and bring the husbands into line. Keep in mind that these were faithful followers of Islam perpetrating such atrocities on other Muslims. Furthermore, in doing so they were acting in compliance with the beliefs of their religion and in full obedience to the teachings of their holy writings.

In another instance, Arafat had the hands of Arab children chopped off in front of their parents. In this case, Arafat ordered the parents of Muslims whom he thought were unfaithful to Allah to be brought before him, along with their young children. When the parents and children were all together, Arafat had several of his followers restrain the parents while others in his group held the children's arms out across a wooden table. The Palestinian leader then ordered his followers to remove the children's hands. Note that this was not a surgical-type removal with a sharp knife, though that would have been bad enough. No, this removal took time. The men actually *sawed* and *hacked* at the hands of these innocent children.[5]

Again, Arafat ordered this act of barbarism to be done to make examples of these people, to keep others "faithful" to Islam, and to bring those individuals whom he thought had strayed from the teachings of Islam back into line. As with his previous act, Arafat was doing this in complete agreement with the teachings of Islam and its holy writings. And as before, he conducted these heinous acts against other Muslims.

Arafat and his group also had a mother and her children murdered on a bus at Jericho—an event that has been repeated many times against innocent people in the Middle East by followers of Islam. When compared to the tortures already described, this seems almost tame. Interestingly, it was Arafat who introduced this type of warfare against children as an act of political terrorism. In May 1974, three of Arafat's PLO members travelled from Lebanon into the northern Israeli town of Ma'alot. There they murdered two parents and a child, whom they found in a home, and then took more than one hundred children hostage at a local school. The members threatened to kill the children if Israel did not release a number of imprisoned PLO terrorists. When Israeli troops attempted a rescue, the members exploded hand grenades and fired on the children, killing twenty-five people—twenty-one of whom were children.[6]

In the Palestinian city of Nablus located in the northern West Bank, Arafat ordered innocent Arabs to be hanged by butcher's hooks under their chins until they died. Just imagine what this torture must have been like. Arafat's men used these king-sized fishhooks to pierce their Muslim brothers under their chins, up through the bottoms of their mouths, and then hoisted their victims up into the air. These poor people were left to flop around like fish in agony until they died. Once again, these acts were conducted by Muslims acting out their faith against other Muslims, whom they believed to not be faithful enough to Islam.[7]

One of the most well-known acts of terrorism committed by Arafat and his group was the murder of eleven Israeli athletes at the Munich Olympics. The group that claimed responsibility for this act was known as Black September, which has been linked to an arm of Arafat's Fatah organization. On the morning of September 5, 1972, eight tracksuit-clad members of the group carrying duffel bags loaded with AKM assault rifles broke into the Olympic Village and used stolen keys to enter the apartments of the Israeli athletes. As the world watched the events unfold on television, the terrorists and hostages were taken by bus to a local airport, where German officials attempted a rescue attempt. In the end, the rescue failed and all eleven athletes were killed.[8]

Here are some other key atrocities that Arafat or members of groups under his command committed during his career as leader of the Palestinian Liberation Organization:

- February 21, 1970: A PLO member bombs SwissAir flight 330 bound for Tel Aviv. Forty-seven people are killed.
- May 8, 1970: PLO terrorists attack an Israeli school bus. Nine children and three teachers are killed.
- September 6, 1970: PLO terrorists hijack TWA, Pan-Am, and BOAC airplanes.
- March 1, 1973: Palestinian terrorists take over the Saudi embassy in Khartoum, killing two Americans and a Belgian.
- April 11, 1974: Palestinian terrorists attack an apartment building in Israel, killing eleven people.
- March 1975: Members of Fatah take hostages in a hotel in Tel Aviv. Three Israeli soldiers and three civilians are killed.
- March 1978: Members of Fatah take over a bus and kill twenty-one Israelis.
- October 7, 1985: Palestinian terrorists hijack the Italian cruise ship *Achille Lauro*, shooting a wheelchair-bound elderly man and throwing him overboard.
- September 6, 1986: Terrorists attack the Neve-Shalom synagogue in Istanbul, killing twenty-two worshipers.
- July/September 2000: Arafat rejects a peace settlement offered by Israeli Prime Minister Ehud Barak and continues to incite, support, and fund terrorism.[9]

These represent just a sampling of the many acts of terrorism Arafat committed during his time on earth. Remember that the slaughtering bomb attacks "invented" by Arafat and the other atrocities committed by his regimes have killed not only Israelis but also Americans and other nationalities in times of peace. As Jeff Jacoby of the *Boston Globe* commented after Arafat's death in November 11, 2004, "It would take an encyclopedia to catalog all of the evil Arafat committed. But that is no excuse for not trying to recall at least some of it. . . . In a better world, the

PLO chief would have met his end on a gallows, hanged for mass murder such as the Nazi chiefs were hanged at Nuremberg."[10]

A FEW POINTS TO REMEMBER

In mentioning these atrocities, it is important to again emphasize that those who conducted these acts were faithful followers of Islam, who were acting according to their beliefs. These individuals felt justified in committing these acts of terror because they had been convinced they were waging a holy war against those who were not a part of the Dar Al Islam. What is especially concerning is that as Islam spreads throughout the world, there is a great risk that we will begin to see more and more of these types of regimes that are set on perpetrating acts of terrorism against all those who do not adhere to the tenets of Islam.

Before we continue on in this study, I feel it is necessary to mention a few key points for us to keep in mind. First, it is important to firmly understand that God loves the men and women who call themselves Muslims. Jesus Christ died not just for the Jews, not just for the Christians, and not just for the atheists, Buddhists, and Hindus, *but also for the Muslims.* As we examine the ways in which these people are acting out against us as our enemies, we must remember that they are trapped in a negative system of thought. In fact, the war that we have been fighting in Iraq, Afghanistan and elsewhere is more a war against the culture of Islam than it is a war against Arab tribe members. There are many Arabs who believe in the God of Abraham, Isaac, and Jacob, and many who trust in Jesus. These people are not our enemies; they are our friends.

Second, it is important to keep in mind exactly whom we are talking about when we refer to various groups within Islamic society. It is not proper to call all the non-Jewish people living in the Middle East "Arabs"; the term "Bedouin" is probably a better word to describe the various people groups. Most non-Jews living in the Middle East and elsewhere have different ethnic backgrounds. What they all share in common is that they adhere to the beliefs and tenets of Islam. In addition, when most people speak of "Arabs" (a people group), they actually mean "Muslims" (adherents to the religion of Islam). The terms are used interchangeably in society today, and the media confuse them. We do not want to fall into that trap.

Third, note that two terms that are often used for the followers of Islam are "Moslem" and "Muslim," although "Muslim" is the preferred term today. According to the Center for Nonproliferation Studies, "Moslem" and "Muslim" are two different spellings for the same word, with the two variations coming about as the result of a difference in transliteration methods (much the way we have two variations of the Chinese capital city "Peking" or "Beijing"). However, the Arabic roots of the two words are different. A "Muslim" in Arabic means "one who gives himself to God," while a "Moslem" in Arabic means "one who is evil and unjust." For this reason, most journalists in recent years have switched to using "Muslim."[11]

There are more misconceptions about Islam connected to Jews and Christians than we can count. As we look at the roots of these during the course of this study, we will often find that these deceptions are deliberate. Every thinking person needs to become aware of these issues, because we will all be confronted with them in the days and years to come. For not only is Islam often the least-understood religion in the world, but it is also the fastest-growing one.

THE GROWTH OF ISLAM WORLDWIDE

In truth, the growth rate of the Islamic religion is staggering. This should be a cause of great concern for Christians, because history has shown that the spread of Islam generally results in the death of the Christian Church. Often this is a literal, real, and painful death for the followers of Christ in the cultures and countries in which Islam takes root. Just think of nations such as Libya, Morocco, Algeria, and Turkey, where Christians are persecuted for attempting to spread the gospel of Christ. Islam is the only religion that has conquered peoples and lands that were once considered part of the Kingdom of Jesus Christ.

To gain a better perspective on what is going on today demographically with Islam and Christianity, consider the following data. Seventy percent of the people in the world whom we would define as "unreached" are Muslims.[12] This number points to a problem within our own culture. Many of those "unreached" peoples are Muslims who live right here in our own communities. Furthermore, there are a significant number of Catholics and Protestants in America today who are

"Cultural Christians"—individuals who claim to be Christians (perhaps because they attend church or mass and claim to lead a "good" life) but do not represent true believers. Many of these people, by not having a workable and personal faith, become easy targets for proselytizing by Muslims or unwittingly give aid to expanding Islam in our society. Don Richardson, author of *The Secrets of the Koran,* states that "anyone in the world who does not become a Christian in the next two decades will probably become a Muslim or at least will have been urged to join Islam ten, fifteen, or twenty times."[13]

In 2002, there were more than 1.2 billion adherents to Islam in more than 165 countries in the world.[14] Islam has a worldwide compound growth rate of 5.9 percent, which is approximately double that of Christianity (at 2.9 percent). Using this growth rate, it can be estimated that the number of adherents to Islam in the world today is in the range of 1.6 billion. Samuel Huntington, a Harvard professor and author of *The Clash of Civilizations and the Remaking of World Order,* believes there will be 5 percent more Muslims than Christians in the world by 2025.[15] In forming his conclusions, Huntington relied on empirical data and was impartial in his findings. All of this information, again, should be of great concern to Christians. In business, we know that if one company is growing twice as fast as another, then that company will be the long-term winner *unless the slower-growing company changes its strategy.*

The Catholic Church just reported there are now more Muslims than Catholics, and some studies show that in five to seven years Islam will be the dominant religion in the world.[16] This is not that much of a stretch considering the demographic trends, mathematical compound rates of growth, and vast sums of money that leaders of Islam are spending in this cultural invasion. For instance, one of the primary goals of Muslim leaders is to convert all of Africa to Islam. Today, we find Muslim missionaries flooding into that continent, and Islamic leaders are encouraging their men to marry Christian women and raise Muslim children. Compare this to the scant 4 percent of evangelical Christian missionaries and monies that are being expended to reach the Muslim world. In many Muslim nations, there are absolutely *no* Christian missionaries—including native-born citizens as well as those from other countries. This is another problem of gigantic proportions.

In the face of these statistics, it is interesting that some Christian commentators still "feel" that Christianity will keep its numerical advantage over Islam. These uninformed individuals seem to be blissfully asleep on the watchtower, unaware of the implications of compound rates of growth. Furthermore, it is apparent that Muslims are extremely committed to their beliefs—much more than Christians in the world today. As Dr. Khalid Al-Mansour, an international lawyer and co-author of the book *The Challenges of Spreading Islam in America,* has noted, "Christians are unwilling to die for their cause. True Muslims want to die every day."[17]

One key Islamic leader has stated, "In fifty years we will capture the western world for Islam." Muslims have declared this century as theirs, and no one can argue that they have certainly dominated the first decade. However, when it comes to understanding the growth of Islam in Western cultures, there are many more factors at work than one might realize. To understand these factors, consider the following demographic information about what is happening in the continent of Europe. This information reveals certain trends that will impact the look of the world during the coming years and change the global culture our children will inherit.

OUR CHANGING WORLD

Researchers tell us that for a culture to maintain itself for twenty-five years, it must have a fertility rate of 2.11 children per family. If the culture has less than a 2.11 fertility rate, it will be in decline.[18] In other words, the parents must produce enough offspring to replace themselves, plus a few more, to sustain that culture. If two sets of parents were to each have only one child, it would mean that there would soon be half as many children as parents in that nation. If those children in turn were to each have only one child, then there would be one-fourth as many grandchildren as grandparents.

History shows that no culture has ever recovered from a 1.9 fertility rate. Furthermore, a fertility rate of 1.3 is *impossible to reverse*. This is because at a rate of 1.3 children per family it would take eighty to one hundred years for the situation to correct itself, and there is no economic model currently in place that could sustain a society for that length of time. If a nation had one million babies born into it in 2006, it would be impossible for it to have two million adults enter the workforce in 2026.[19]

This is exactly what we find in Europe today. A quick glance at the dismal fertility rates of the countries in Europe serves as a reminder of the decline of those societies and cultures:

- France: 1.8
- England: 1.6
- Greece: 1.3
- Germany: 1.3
- Italy: 1.2
- Spain: 1.1

When you factor in the combined fertility rates of all the thirty-one countries in the European Union, you find an average rate of 1.38. As stated above, historical research indicates that these cultures cannot recover from such a low fertility rate and that these numbers are impossible to reverse. In a matter of years, Europe should cease to exist.

However, the population of Europe is not declining; it is *growing.* How can this be? The reason is because of Islamic immigration. Since 1990, approximately 90 percent of all immigrants into Europe have been from Islamic nations. Consider France, for example. As noted above, the fertility rate for that nation is 1.8 percent. However, the fertility rate among Muslims is 8.1 percent. It is the Muslims who are accounting for the real population increase in this country.

Only a generation ago, the region of southern France consisted of a very "churched" Christian population. Today, there are more mosques in this area than there are churches. Furthermore, statistics show that 30 percent of the children in France age twenty and younger are Islamic. In the larger cities, including Nice, Marseilles, and Paris, 45 percent of the children age twenty and younger are Muslim. By 2027 (at the latest), one in five Frenchmen will be Muslim; and by 2046, France will be an Islamic republic.

We see similar trends in other European nations. During the last thirty years, the Muslim population of Great Britain has grown from 82,000 to more than 2.5 million. Muslims, using profits obtained from oil money, are buying abandoned Anglican churches across the country and converting them into mosques. In 1993, there were only 150 mosques in England, but by 2003 that number had grown to more than 1,100. There are now more active mosques in Great Britain than there are active churches, and there are more Muslims than there are evangelical Christians.

In the Netherlands, 50 percent of all newborns are Muslim, and experts believe that in fifteen years or less one half of the entire population will be Muslim. In Russia, there are more than 23 million Muslims. Given Russia's current population, that means that one out of every five Russians is a Muslim. In just a few short years, 40 percent of the Russian army will be comprised of Islamic believers. Due to high birth rates and immigration into the country, Islam is poised to become the primary religion in Russia by 2050. As one Russian mourned, "Centuries-old mosques are being replaced by modern, Wahhabi-built mosques. Old imams who survived the communists are being replaced by Wahhabi clerics. This is not only true for predominantly Muslim countries like Tajikistan, but also for autonomous regions inside Russia like Bashkiria and Tatarstan, where most people consider themselves more Russian than Muslim."[20]

In Belgium, 25 percent of the population and 50 percent of newborns are Muslims. These figures led the government to conclude that by 2025 one-third of all European children will be born into Muslim families. Likewise, Walter Radermacher, vice president of Germany's Federal Statistical Office, recently stated, "The fall in the [German] population can no longer be stopped. Its downward spiral is irreversible."[21] There are at least 52 million Muslims in Europe, and that number is expected to double to 104 million within the next twenty years.

Perhaps Muammar al-Gaddafi, the de facto leader of Libya since a coup in 1969, summed it up best: "There are signs that Allah will grant victory to Islam in Europe without swords, without guns, without conquest. We don't need terrorists, we don't need homicide bombers. The fifty-plus-million Muslims [in Europe] will turn it into a Muslim continent within a few decades."[22]

As we consider all of this information, it is important for us to remember that Islam is more than just a religion. In fact, it is a form of cultural imperialism in which its leaders attempt to impose the rules and regulations of seventh-century Arabia on modern times. In this sense, Islam is a force in the world that is unrivalled in the course of human history. As we will see in the next chapter, this force is not isolated to just nations in Europe, Asia, Africa, or in the Middle East. The subtle influence and spread of Islam can be seen in countries throughout the world, including the United States.

FOR STUDY AND REFLECTION

At this point, if you have the opportunity, I suggest you view the short, five-minute introduction to *Jihad in America*. You can find the video online at youtube.com or on Google videos at http://video.google.com/videoplay?docid=-9172967809538239506#.

Consider the following questions based on the material you read in this chapter:

1. According to the opening section of *Jihad in America*, the documentary produced in 1994 by Steven Emerson in concert with the FBI, the CIA, and the State Department, what is the single greatest threat to America's survival? What did the experts determine was the best way to overcome that threat?

2. What does the term *jihad* mean? Why is it an important duty for Muslims? Why are so many Muslims willing to end their lives in suicide bombings, in what they believe is an act of jihad?

3. How many groups of people are there in the Islamic universe? Can there ever be peace between the groups? Why or why not?

4. What are some of the atrocities Yasser Arafat committed against his own people (other Muslims)? Why were these actions acceptable according to the Koran?

5. Why is it incorrect to believe that Christianity will maintain its numerical advantage in the world over Islam in the coming decades? What is the stated goal of many Muslim leaders today as it relates to the spread of Islam?

6. Why must a culture maintain a fertility rate of 2.11 to survive? What is the issue that we see in Europe today as it relates to population growth and the spread of Islam?

CHAPTER TWO

THE CULTURAL WAR

PERHAPS YOU ARE saying to yourself that this could never happen in America. After all, our nation was built on Christian principles, and today America is one of the most Christianized countries on earth. In fact, 78 percent of Americans identify themselves as Christians (roughly 51 percent Protestant and 25 percent Catholic), and non-Christian religions, including Buddhism, Hinduism, Islam, and Judaism, collectively make up only 3.9 to 5.5 percent of the population.[1]

However, as we have seen in Europe, Africa, and the rest of the world, the growth rate of Islam is expanding in America at an exponential rate. Currently, it is reportedly at 13.94 percent, and the number of Muslims now stands at somewhere between fourteen million to twenty million.[2] When you consider the fact that in 1970 there were 100,000 Muslims in the United States, this is quite an increase—and researchers believe the Muslim population *doubled* from 2000 to 2005. Even if we assume the lower number of fourteen million to be correct, if the growth rate continues at 13.94 percent, there would be 112 million Muslims in the United States by 2020. This could make evangelical Christians a minority in the nation.

In the year 2000, Islam was numerically equal to Judaism as America's largest minority religion. However, statistics now reveal that Muslims outnumber Jews by a ratio of two to one. The data also indicate that there are more Muslims in the United States than there are Episcopalians, more Muslims than there are Presbyterians, and many more Muslims than there are Nazarenes.[3]

The United States Immigration Service tells us that approximately 100,000 legal Muslim immigrants are allowed into the country each year.[4] Many illegal Islamic immigrants also slip into the country. As is the case with the African missionaries, all of these immigrants to the United States are encouraged to marry Christian women and raise Muslim children. The largest immigrant Islamic population resides in Dearborn, Michigan, where more than 30 percent of the adult population is comprised of Muslims from other countries.[5]

Furthermore, in 2000 there were 1,400 mosques in the United States, while today there are at least 2,000.[6] What is interesting to note is that only a few of these structures were purposely built to serve as mosques. The rest were converted from other types of buildings—including abandoned churches. We also see this trend occurring in Great Britain.

The CIA, FBI, and various Islamic organizations claim that 24 percent of the Muslims in America are Black Muslims. A study conducted by Johns Hopkins and the American University state that Black Muslims number 33 percent of the total. If the population of Muslims in United States is at seven million, it would mean that the number of Black Muslims in the country numbers somewhere between 1.68 million and 2.3 million.[7] (Note this data is from the year 2000, so the actual numbers may be significantly higher). Currently, there are 818,900 men of African-American descent in jail or in prisons in the United States. Sadly, 195,500 of these inmates are between the ages of eighteen and twenty-four.[8] The positive and hopeful counterpoint to this is that there are 465,000 men of African-American descent between the ages of eighteen and twenty-four who are enrolled in colleges. In a later chapter, we will examine how perhaps the cruelest and most arrogant hoax perpetrated on the black community is the deception of these Black Muslims.

In the previous chapter, we examined the fertility rates of various countries in Europe and made the statement that it takes a birth rate of 2.11 to sustain a culture. In Canada, the fertility rate is currently at 1.6 percent. As in Europe, Islam is the fastest-growing religion in that country. From 2001 to 2006, the population of Canada grew by 1.6 million, of which 1.2 million were immigrants, and most of those immigrants were Muslims. In the United States, the fertility rate is also at 1.6 percent. However, with the Latino population factored into the results, it stands at 2.11. As we discussed, that number is the bare minimum necessary to sustain a culture.

Perhaps you are still saying to yourself that things are not so bad in America. After all, you might have heard that in 2007 more than 23,000 students on college campuses in the United States made faith commitments. The only problem is that these students committed themselves—on U.S. campuses at U.S. schools—to Allah, the God of Islam. As Christians, this should reveal to us that one of the most readily identifiable forces we are fighting today in the cultural war is Islam.[9] As we will see in this chapter, proponents of this religion have been quite successful in advancing their agenda in Western culture, often in subtle ways.

A POLICY OF TOLERANCE

One of the primary ways that Islam is becoming embedded in Western culture is through politically correct policies supposedly promoting "tolerance" for different viewpoints. In many countries, such as Australia, Canada, France, and other nations in Europe, speaking the truth about Islam, if it is perceived as a negative against a group of people, is an offense punishable by jail or fines. It is also a crime to preach the gospel of Christ if one implies that other systems of thought or religion are inadequate. However, it is perfectly acceptable to criticize Christianity or Judaism. The regulations that permit this travesty are referred to as "hatred laws."

One example of how officials have enforced these laws occurred a few years ago in France. As mentioned previously, there are now more Muslims in France than there are evangelical Christians (a fact that sheds some light on why France is always opposed to actions against Islamic regimes). On April 15, 2008, Brigitte Bardot, one of France's most famous international film stars of the 1950 and 1960s, went on trial for the fifth time on the charge of "inciting racial hatred."

On this occasion, Bardot had written a letter to the Interior Minister of France, in which she stated, "I am fed up with being under the thumb of this [Muslim] population, which is destroying us, destroying our country, and imposing its habits." She had also lamented about the "Islamitization" of France. For her comments, the courts fined her 15,000 Euros (the equivalent of $23,760 U.S. dollars at the time) and handed down a two-month prison sentence, which was suspended only because of her health. The prosecutor in the case, Anne de Fontette, told the court, "I am a little tired of prosecuting Mrs. Bardot."[10] Of course, there would have been no fine or sentence if Bardot had instead chosen to criticize Judaism, Christianity, Buddhism, Hinduism, or even the atheists living in her county.

In England, the home secretary banned right-wing Dutch parliamentarian Geert Wilders from entering the country for "inciting religious hatred," which is forbidden by law in Britain. Wilders has made such statements as, "Where Islam sets root, freedom dies," and has been critical of allowing Muslims to immigrate. In the United States, he met with resistance from groups who attempted to block two scheduled lectures at Temple University and Columbia University. Wilders currently lives under police protection because of death threats. Again, there would have been no uproar against Wilders if he had made comments criticizing Christianity or Judaism.[11]

What is especially chilling is that Hillary Clinton pushed for similar laws to be put in place in this country when her husband was President of the United States. And, in a sense, these laws do exist here in a de facto sense. Although they have not been officially enacted in this country, saying negative (though truthful) things about Islam is forbidden at many colleges, universities, corporations, and media outlets across the country. Furthermore, as is the case in the countries that have officially adopted the hatred laws, speaking the truth in a positive sense about Judaism or Christianity is also not welcome and, in fact, is sometimes met with a *very harsh* response. In many cases, truth no longer seems to be the standard of measurement when it comes to evaluating what is right and what is wrong.

We see a similar phenomenon occurring in the media. On September 16, 2004, a radical Islamic group led by Abu Musab al-Zarqawi kidnapped an American contractor named Eugene Armstrong. On September 20, 2004, the group filmed the beheading of Armstrong in an act of religious ritual, calling him a "Christian dog." However, when the *New York Times* wrote about the event, the editors dropped the words "Christian dog" from the report. Likewise, in a series of reports in 2005 on suicide bombings in Jerusalem, the Reuters news agency never mentioned anything about the victims of the attacks or their families, though it did report on the suffering of the murderers' families. As Amnon Rubenstein of *The Jerusalem Post* notes, "Western forces play a major—albeit unintended—role in transforming what the Islamists are doing into something normative."[12]

This "normalizing" of Islamic culture occurs in more subtle ways as well. On March 27, 2005, Ed Bradley narrated a piece for *60 Minutes* in which the network praised the Saudi Arabians for their upcoming "election." What the reporters left out was the fact that Saudi Arabia has no political parties, no real constitution, and no legislature. In fact, the population can only vote for about half of the appointments on the slate—the other half are appointments selected by the Saud family, which has ruled the nation with an iron fist since 1932. Women are not permitted to vote at all, which is not surprising given the fact that they are required to wear *chadors* (long black robes with hoods and slits for eyes), are not permitted to drive, and are generally relegated to second-class status in the nation.[13] Christians cannot build a church in Saudi Arabia or even pray openly, and no Jew can set foot in the country—not if he or she wants to live.

ATTACK ON THE EDUCATION SYSTEM

Another avenue by which Islamic doctrine is spread in the United States is through the education system. Again, much of the problem stems from the attempts of well-meaning teachers and administrators to "broaden" their students' minds about other cultures. In California, for example, seventh graders are required to take a course in Islam, in which they are encouraged to dress like Muslims, take Muslim names, and even plan a pilgrimage to Mecca.

What is more, these young people are told to plan a *jihad* or holy war and pray to "Allah the Merciful." The prayer the students are taught to pray, called the *Shahadah*, is the one a person prays when becoming a Muslim. However, the students are not allowed to read the Bible or to pray to the God of the Bible in school. Schools in other states (most recently in Virginia) are following this curriculum. Imagine the uproar that would occur if children in school were forced to pray to ask Jesus Christ into their lives.

In England, two boys at Alsager High School were punished for refusing to kneel on prayer mats and worship Allah during a class demonstration on Islam. According to a Fox News report, irate parents said that a religious education teacher told the students to wear Muslim headgear during these lessons. One grandfather was quoted as saying, "If Muslims were asked to go to church on Sunday and take Holy Communion there would be war."[14]

Some people may think that the cultural war is far away from their daily lives here in America. Yet, while we have thousands of our young men and women serving overseas, the U.S. Immigration Service tells us that each day there are many people of Middle Eastern descent, with alleged questionable motives, sneaking into the country across the Mexican/U.S. border. If this number is one thousand, one hundred, ten or even one, we have a bigger problem on our hands than we realize.

Of course, due to our education system, Muslim infiltrators don't need to sneak across our borders—we let them in without so much as a thought about the implications. Every year, Saudi Arabia spends hundreds of millions of dollars to pay for tens of thousands of Muslim men to come to U.S. colleges. Once again, the goal is for these men to stay in this country, marry a non-Muslim woman, convert her to Islam, have as many children as possible, and then raise them as Muslims.

Saudi Arabia and other Islamic countries have been engaging in an aggressive campaign of endowing political science departments and international studies departments at U.S. colleges and universities. This funding allows these nations to gain inroads into these schools and fill these departments with Islamic professors. Once in place, these professors propagandize and proselytize American students, encouraging them to embrace Islam while teaching them to hate America, Christians, and Jews.

The Islamic infiltration has even spread to military institutions such as West Point. In October 2006, the United States Army built a new mosque after Muslim leaders complained that the office where cadets gathered for Friday prayers had become too crowded. In recent years, the Army has been actively recruiting cadets from Muslim countries such as Afghanistan and Saudi Arabia, and Muslim enrollment at West Point has increased from two in 2001 to thirty-two in 2006. In dedicating the new mosque, the Army was clearly following the lead of the Marines, who dedicated their mosque at Quantico, Virginia, in June 2006. Paul Sperry, an expert on terror, stated that "with the Quantico mosque, the Pentagon is facilitating the study of the holy text the enemy uses, heretically or not, as their manual of warfare."[15]

Perhaps Omar Achmad, head of the Council on American-Islamic Relations (CAIR), best summed up the intent of these efforts to infiltrate American academia when he said, "Islam isn't in America to be equal to any other faiths, but to become dominant. The Koran, the Muslim book of scripture, should be the highest authority in America, and Islam the only accepted religion on earth."[16]

THE FETHULLAH GÜLEN COMMUNITY

In recent years, charter schools have been especially useful to those who wish to spread an Islamic agenda in the United States. Charter schools are publicly funded but are not subject to the same rules that govern other public schools. Instead, they are required to achieve certain goals as outlined in the school's charter. Most of these schools specialize in fields such as mathematics and the sciences, but at least one group also promotes an Islamic agenda. These particular schools, which have innocent-sounding names such as Chicago Math and Science Academy and Pioneer Charter School of Science, educate up to 35,000 students in one hundred institutions and comprise the largest charter school network in the United States.

During the past ten years, the schools in this network have brought in thousands of educators from Turkey, most of them having ties to a Turkish Muslim named Fethullah Gülen. For this reason, the schools in this network have become known as the "Fethullah Gülen Community" or FGC. FGC schools are unique in that unlike other religious schools in the United States, they promote a religious agenda (an Islamic one) but still receive public funding.

Although there has been little public discussion (or even reports in the media) about FGC schools, each year more and more U.S. tax dollars have gone to establish and fund these institutions. Most of these schools claim little or no affiliation with one another, but they do have some striking similarities, including chronic problems with special education compliance, a high teacher turnover rate, a high usage of visas to fill staffing needs, numerous on-campus Turkish cultural activities (such as Turkish clubs, Turkish "Olympiads," and class trips to Anatolian or Turkish festivals), and school-sponsored trips to Turkey.

What is especially alarming is that according to Turkish scholar Bayram Balci, the founder of these schools, Fethullah Gülen, established these institutions to bring about a "universal caliphate" ruled by Islamic law.[17] Graham Fuller, a former CIA agent, also notes that Gülen is leading "one of the most important movements in the Muslim world today."[18] In fact, Gülen's own followers have referred to him as a "contemporary Islam's Billy Graham."[19]

Gülen, whose beliefs are connected to Sufism (a mystical form of Islam), began his career in 1957 when he was appointed to serve at a mosque in Edirene, Turkey. Once there, he learned of the teachings of Said-i-Nursi, a Kurdish preacher who believed that Muslims should engage modernity to promote the spread of Islam. Gülen put these beliefs into practice in 1966 when he was transferred to a mosque in Ismir. From this location, he began establishing a network of student boarding houses, private schools, residences, and later, universities to further his goal of spreading Islam to the world. Gülen referred to this network of schools as a *hizmet* movement, which is one of the highest duties in Islam and implies both religious and national service. He called his community of followers the *cemaat,* and he is referred to as their *hocaefendi* (master lord).

Gülen soon expanded his network through countries in the former Soviet Union and into the Balkans.[20] In 1997 he moved to the United States and began making inroads into the West. Although his residency was initially denied because the Department of Homeland Security did not deem him to be an expert in the field of education (his formal education is limited to five years of elementary school), Gülen was able to ultimately gain permanent residency with the help of several CIA agents.[21] Once his visa was approved, he moved to southeastern Pennsylvania and began building his charter schools in the United States.

Today, the Gülen Movement has even spread into politics. The FGC is known to have supported the election campaigns of certain U.S. politicians, and these politicians have returned the favor by appearing at various FGC events. In September 2007, for instance, Secretary of State Hillary Clinton attended a Ramadan breakfast organized by the Gülenist Turkish Cultural Center in New York City.[22]

THE ISLAMIC SAUDI ACADEMY

As if this were not shocking enough, there is a preparatory school in Alexandria, Virginia, called the Islamic Saudi Academy. This school is accredited with the Southern Association of Colleges and Universities, is a member of the Northern Virginia Independent Athletic Conference, and has a chapter of the National Honor Society. The school supports the Mount Vernon Youth Athletic Association, holds an annual science fair and Shakespearean drama program, and takes part in the Model United Nations program, the presidential classroom program, and Future Business Leaders of America. At the surface level, the school seems like an ideal place for students to attend.

However, the academy has repeatedly been accused of promoting terrorism. Susan L. Douglas, a former social studies teacher at the school, authored several textbooks for the International Institute of Islamic Thought—an organization that was raided in 2002 by the FBI because of suspected terrorist links. In 2005, one of the academy's most vaunted graduates—the class valedictorian of 1999—was convicted on charges of providing material support to the al-Qaeda terrorist network. The conviction led New York Senator Charles Schumer to issue a press release questioning whether the school was another *madrassa*—a term for an Arabic school that teaches radical Islamic theology. In addition, the director of the academy was arrested on June 9, 2008, for failing to report child abuse allegations (which are acceptable in Islam) and for obstruction of justice.

In October 2007, the U.S. Commission on International Religious Freedom urged the State Department to shut down the school on the grounds that it taught religious intolerance that could prove to be a danger to the United States. The commission found that the textbooks contained passages condoning intolerance, murder of adulterers, and killing those who left Islam or encouraged others to do so. The school promised to remove the offensive passages from their textbooks, but when the commission again investigated in June 2008, it found that the academy had not removed the material. At the time of this writing, the school remains open and is happy to review the application of anyone who wants to attend.[23]

NOT A THREAT?

The biggest difficulty I often find with our education system is that students, teachers, and administrators are, as a rule, not well educated about Islam. Because of this unawareness, they fall prey to the terrible mistruths taught in the name of Islam. To compound the problem, I find that most of the books on the shelves in major bookstores make statements and claims about Islam without substance or corroboration. The authors of these works often engage in outright lies and pseudo-intellectual approaches in their thinly disguised support for Islam. This is done in the name of diversity and tolerance, but it is intellectually dishonest. These authors have to make these claims because they do not have the facts in their favor. You can almost see the cultural war going on right there on the bookshelves at Borders.

For this reason, I suggest you take a close look at the resource list at the end of this book. These books are not easy to find, and you will likely have to order them online because most bookstores, even in this time of war, stock only politically correct books on Islam, which have more misinformation and half-truths than anything else. I should also mention this warning: be careful if you use the Internet to research facts about Islam. Some of the sites from Islamic providers send out powerful viruses when you access them that fly under the radar of all but the most sophisticated virus software. I contracted several computer viruses while doing research for this book and had to have them professionally removed. One of the worst was a key logger virus that started sending everything I keyed into my computer to a remote location in a foreign country.

It is my goal that by the end of this study you will know enough about the truth behind Islam to understand the claims and secret agendas behind many of the educational efforts discussed in this chapter. You will be able to help when the time comes. In addition, as we continue our study, I think you will find that we are dealing with both cultural and religious issues. While we may touch on the political issues, it is important to note that these originate from the underlying spiritual issues. We will review these in greater depth in later chapters, but first I think it is important to understand how we got into this mess and how the religion of Islam began.

For Study and Reflection

Consider the following questions based on the material you read in this chapter:

1. The popular culture in America has given us many "facts" we have come to believe about Islam. Some people call these myths, while others believe them to be the truth. List ten common beliefs about Islam.

    1.

    2.

    3.

    4.

    5.

    6.

    7.

    8.

    9.

    10.

2. What conclusions can you draw from the statistics at the beginning of this chapter about the growth rate of Islam in America? About the growth rate of Islam in Canada?

3. What are "hatred" laws? Why were these laws put into place in countries in Europe? What have been the side effects as they relate to the growth of Islam?

4. Why is it often not acceptable in U.S. institutions to speak positively about Christianity and Judaism? Why is it not acceptable to speak negatively (even if it is the truth) about Islam?

5. What is often at the root of teachers' and administrators' decision to teach about Islam in schools? How has this enabled the infiltration of Islamic doctrine in American schools?

6. What is the danger with allowing a school such as the Islamic Saudi Academy to exist in this country?

During the course of this study, we will look at many cultural impressions and try to discover which are true and which are false. Pray for wisdom and understanding as we examine the religion and culture of Islam and contrast it with faith in the God of Abraham, Isaac, and Jacob. Also, be sure to review the list of helpful resources on Islam included in the back of this book.

CHAPTER THREE

THE STRANGE ORIGINS OF ISLAM

SINCE 2003, I HAVE spoken many times about Islam in various settings. Invariably, someone from the law enforcement community will be in the audience and come up to see me afterward. They agree that what I have said is true, but they tell me that I am understating the case. To me, this is incredible. *I have just finished telling them that Islam is the greatest threat facing the world today, and they tell me that the problem is greater than I am stating!* These law enforcement officials then proceed to tell me details of training and operations that reveal even further just what a great threat Islam is to this nation. When you add it all up, you can only conclude that something is very wrong with this picture.

All of this may cause you to wonder how we got into this mess. How did Islam get a foothold in our culture? How did it spread from Saudi Arabia and the Middle East to the rest of the world? And what has caused the religion to have such incredible growth rates among populations worldwide? This is a complicated issue that has developed over a number of years. To help us understand the problem, we need to go back and examine the strange origins of Islam and then look at some important watershed events that have been a factor in its rise in the world.

MUHAMMAD'S FIRST REVELATION

Muhammad ibn 'Abdullah was born in AD 570 into the Quaraysh tribe in Mecca.[1] Mecca at the time was a major center on a caravan route that paralleled the Red Sea in western Arabia. The Quaraysh tribe worshiped the moon god and was in charge of guarding a big black stone at the Ka'aba. The Ka'aba itself was a cube-like temple filled with 360 idols and located near a sacred spring known as Zamzam. Muhammad's father was Abd-Allah, and one of his uncles was Obied-Allah. If this name "Allah" sounds familiar, it is because it was a common practice in ancient civilizations to include the name of one's deity in the family name.

Muhammad helped lead one of Mecca's caravans. At the age of twenty-five, he married Khadija, a woman fifteen years older than he. Khadija was the owner of the largest caravan in the region, which made her a very prominent woman in Mecca. For Muhammad, the marriage proved to be a good economic move; it afforded him the luxury of not having to work to sustain himself. Muhammad remained married to Khadija alone for twenty-five years until her death around AD 635.

Many scholars believe that Muhammad had a medical problem, which modern researchers and physicians believe was a form of epilepsy. He often went into the mountains and caves alone to meditate, where he sometimes had seizures. During these dramatic events, Muhammad would fall to the ground, his eyes would roll back in his head, and he would shake and froth at the mouth as he thrashed about on the ground.

Around the year AD 610, when Muhammad was forty years old, he had one of these seizures in a cave on Mount Hira, just outside the city of Mecca. However, this time the seizures were accompanied by visions and strange voices. Muhammad claimed he was visited by the angel Gabriel, whom he said appeared to him on behalf of the same God the Jews and Christians worshiped. The angel commanded him to read, to which the illiterate Muhammad replied that he could not. The angel squeezed Muhammad and commanded him again to read, to which Muhammad replied that he could not. After this, the angel squeezed him to within an inch of his life and commanded him to read once more. It is at this point that Muslims believe the first Sura of the Koran was revealed to Muhammad.

After the episode, Muhammad was understandably frightened and confused about what had happened. He began to worry that he had been possessed by demons or that he was simply going crazy. Returning home to Mecca, he related the events to his wife and confessed his fear that he had somehow become a sorcerer or had gone mad. "I had a seizure in a cave," he said to her. "I fell down on the floor, my eyes rolled back in my head, and I shook as I often do. But this time I heard strange voices. Am I crazy, or am I a prophet?"

At this point, we must put ourselves in the place of Muhammad's wife. She was fifty-five years old, and he was forty. Although she knew he had been enjoying the benefits of her money, she probably worried that she didn't look as good to him as she did fifteen years ago when they were first married. The people of Mecca lived in a very harsh desert environment, and people aged quickly under those conditions. Perhaps you remember the picture of the beautiful, young Afghan girl who appeared on the cover of *National Geographic* magazine during the first Gulf War. She had piercing blue-green eyes and was the epitome of beauty in the Middle East. However, fifteen years later when photographers found her again, the effects of living in the wilds and desert had taken their toll. She still had the same piercing blue-green eyes, but, as one observer unkindly stated, it looked as if she had turned into the "sea hag" popularized in children's cartoons some years ago.

Khadija was *twenty years older* than this poor girl from Afghanistan. Can you imagine what she must have looked like after the ravages of the climate had taken their toll on her? Also, picture her situation. She was living in a violent culture, where beheading was a common practice. If her husband became upset with her and killed her, nobody would care. If she told Muhammad that he was crazy, and her assessment of his condition proved to be correct, then he would kill her anyway. However, if she said something positive, then she would probably live. Given her few options, she decided to console Muhammad and reassure him that he had not gone mad.

At this point you may be wondering how Muhammad had even heard about the angel Gabriel. Remember that Mecca was at the center of a trade route, and Khadija was the owner of the largest caravan in the area. The caravans brought people of different religions into the area and allowed the Meccans to learn something about their religious practices. Two of the main groups with whom the people of Mecca were in constant contact were the Jews and the Christians. Muhammad and Khadija had learned that both groups held an angel named Gabriel in high regard.

Khadija had an uncle who had read the Bible and converted to Christianity, and she and Muhammad decided to visit him where he lived in the desert. After Khadija's uncle listened to Muhammad's story, he decided to conspire with Khadija and tell Muhammad that he must be a prophet. The two told him that it was indeed the angel Gabriel who had spoken to him, and that this made him not only the most recent but also the greatest prophet who ever lived. As you can imagine, Muhammad liked their explanation.

MUHAMMAD'S EARLY CAREER AS A PROPHET

During the time of Muhammad, pagans comprised the largest religious group in Mecca. Some of these groups worshiped the sun, some worshiped the *dabran* (a cluster of five stars), some worshiped the jinns (or demons), some worshiped the Greek goddess Venus, and some worshiped an entity called Sohail. Many of the pagans, as previously mentioned, revered the black stone at the Ka'aba and filled the temple with their idols.

With the confidence gained from his wife's and her uncle's encouragement, Muhammad began to visit these Arab groups and tell them about the voices he was hearing. He claimed that he was the greatest prophet who had ever lived and that they should listen to what he had to say. You can imagine how this might have gone over. Muhammad told the people his story of how he had been in the hills and suffered fits of shaking and rolling on the ground. Then he told them he had heard voices and seen visions. He topped it off by explaining the reason he believed he was the greatest prophet to ever live: his wife and her uncle had told him it was so.

Surely, their first response must have been to say, "Muhammad, we know you. You married the richest woman in town, and you haven't worked *a day in your life since then.*" They told him he was crazy and to go away. Only a few Meccans became his followers, and these consisted of three primary groups: (1) Muhammad's family members and sons of great merchants, (2) people who had fallen out of the first rank in their tribe or had failed to attain it, and (3) weak and unprotected foreigners. Eventually, in AD 622, the city's hostility forced Muhammad to flee with his few followers to Medina, another caravan stop located some two hundred miles north of Mecca. This represented a great setback for the self-proclaimed prophet.

In Medina, Muhammad became an arbiter of disputes. In this role, he sought to ingratiate himself not only with the Arabs but also with the large number of Jews residing in the city. Seeking to confirm his status as the world's greatest prophet, he decided to go to this Jewish population and tell them about the voices he was hearing. Surely, he thought, this more educated group of people would recognize that he displayed the signs of being a true prophet of God, and they would acknowledge his newly elevated status.

The Jews, however, believed he was deluded. When they heard him explain what the angel had supposedly said to him, they referred him to Isaiah 8:20, which states, "'Check their predictions against my testimony,' says the Lord. 'If their predictions are different from mine, it is because there is no light or truth in them'" (NLT). They explained to Muhammad that he was wrong on a number of issues that related to their sacred writings called the Tanakh, which we call the Old Testament, and a true prophet would never go against their sacred book. They, like the pagan groups in Mecca, told him that he was crazy.

This incensed Muhammad, so he decided to go to the Christians he knew, hoping they would be more enlightened than the Jews and realize he had become the greatest prophet to have ever lived. The Christians replied much the same as the Jews. They listened to what he had to say and to his explanation of what the voices had allegedly told him. After they had considered his story, they said, "Muhammad, this just doesn't agree with what we see in the Tanakh or in the teachings of Jesus." To make matters worse, they referred him to the same verse the Jews had used: Isaiah 8:20. They also said he was crazy and told him to get lost.

Muhammad never forgot the intensely consuming anger he felt toward the Jews and the Christians. He referred to them as "The People of the Book" because as far as he was concerned, the Jews and the Christians used the same book when they disputed his claims. The fact that they refuted what he had to say by reading something *out of a book* also angered him because he was illiterate. Muhammad could not even write his own name. The humiliation he felt forever fueled his white-hot hatred against the Christians and the Jews.

What is surprising is that as time passed, more and more of the people in Medina began to follow him. We have seen a similar psychological phenomenon occur in other cultures. For example, during the 1930s, Adolf Hitler and his Nazi party were able to rise to power in Germany by playing on people's fears after an economic depression hit the nation. Ultimately, from 1939 to 1945, Hitler and his SS systematically killed between eleven million and fourteen million people, including about six million Jews.[2] The bigger the lie, it would seem, the easier it was to believe.

MUHAMMAD'S CONQUESTS

After Muhammad's first wife, Khadija, died, he started his life of banditry from Medina. Yes, you heard that right: Muhammad was a bandit. After Muhammad and his followers immigrated to Medina, the Arabs in Mecca began to seize their property; and so, having no means of financial support, they began to raid Meccan caravans. We might also note that the death of Khadija seems to be somewhat shrouded in mystery. No one is quite sure about the circumstances surrounding her death. However, all researchers agree on one point: Muhammad was the primary inheritor of her wealth. This fact has led some scholars to speculate that Khadija's death might not have resulted from natural causes.

Muhammad began his attacks in AD 623, when he was fifty-three years old. He also began attacking everyone else he could find, giving them the choice of either converting to his religion and rule (and paying tribute) or dying. He called his new religion "Islam," which translates into English as "submission." The name referred to the strength that characterized a desert warrior who, when faced with impossible odds, would fight to the death for his tribe.

During that same year, the voices Muhammad heard in his head told him to begin *jihad*, or holy war, against those who refused to join his cause. As mentioned previously, Muhammad divided all peoples into two groups: (1) the Dar Al Islam ("House of Peace"), which included all the faithful followers of Islam, and (2) the Dar Al Harb ("House of War"), which included everyone else. The voices told

Muhammad that this holy war would only end when the members of the Dar Al Islam killed or converted all of the Dar Al Harb to the Islamic faith. If it seems strange that Muhammad would call his followers the "House of Peace" when they were the ones inciting the violence, you have to realize that this is the norm in Islam. As we continue in this study, we will encounter many such contradictory and circuitous concepts and thought processes within the religion.

After the death of Khadija, Muhammad married two women at the same time: Sawda and Aisha. Muhammad's choice of Aisha for a wife surprised even his own followers, as she was only six years old. Can you just imagine them saying, "Muhammad, I know we are a bloodthirsty and greedy bunch of guys, but come on—*six* years old?" Yet, though they were uncomfortable with the arrangement at first, they soon got used to the idea and even incorporated it into their customs. Today, the practice of Muslim men marrying preadolescent girls, as well as those just out of the stage of infancy, continues in some of the more fundamental Islamic countries.

Altogether, Muhammad had sixteen wives, two concubines and four mistresses—but who's counting? He obtained these wives from the people whom he and his followers conquered and pillaged. Muhammad also rewarded his bandits with women, but he allowed them to have only four wives each. When some of them wanted more, he included this limit in the Koran: "If ye fear that ye will not deal fairly by the orphans, marry of the women, who seem good to you, two or three or four; and if ye fear that ye cannot do justice (to so many) then one (only) or (the captives) that your right hands possess" (Sura 4:3). Of course, because Muhammad was Allah's prophet, he didn't feel the rule applied to him.

Muhammad eventually succeeded in raising an army by rewarding his bandits with money and women. He and his "religion" of Islam attracted the misfits from the other tribes in the area. He proved to be a successful conquering bandit king who cleverly used his invented religion for his own political agenda. From AD 623 to 631, he attacked all the tribes who refused to follow him politically or accept Islam, and he demanded that his followers pay a tax to him every year. He was satisfied as long as he received his taxes and the people followed both his cultural and religious edicts.

For the people of the region, opposing Muhammad involved risks that most were not willing to take. If they fought against Muhammad and lost, he would make virtual sex slaves out of their wives and daughters, and their young sons would also become his slaves. The warriors who fought against Muhammad and were captured would be killed by unpleasant means—often right in front of their families. In addition, the Muslims would take all of their money, livestock, and goods. On the other hand, if they agreed to follow Muhammad, all they had to do was follow his customs and pay a yearly tax. The men could have four wives each, and they would share in the booty from other tribes they conquered.

For these misfits in the region, this was a no-brainer. To their way of thinking, they could join Muhammad, have four wives each (whom they could replace any time), and have all the plunder and food they wanted. Furthermore, because Muhammad now held most of the area under his control, even if they were able to successfully resist the members of the Dar Al Islam, it would mean that they would have to toil under harsh conditions in the desert until they died (and be stuck with the same wife who aged as they did). History tells us that by AD 630, many tribes had capitulated to Muhammad's rule.

FINAL VICTORIES

In that same year, Muhammad made preparations to launch an attack against Mecca. He advanced against Mecca with an enormous force, said to number more than ten thousand men, and took the city with few casualties. At this point, most of the Meccans converted to Islam and destroyed the statues of the pagan gods in the Ka'aba. Muhammad was finally able to take control of the temple and the large black stone inside, which was a great prize for him. This large rock is still a great trophy in the world of Islam, and it is still located in the Ka'aba in Mecca, the holiest city of Islam.

In AD 632, Muhammad sent the leaders of some of his various groups of raiders to rule the areas he had conquered and ensure the collection of his tribute. In AD 633, he gave a final public speech that he called the "Sermon on Mount Arafat," which bears a striking resemblance to Jesus' "Sermon on the Mount." (Muhammad liked to cobble together other religious or political systems that he thought he could use, and having heard of Jesus' famous sermon, he wanted to do Him one better.) In this speech, Muhammad told his followers, "After today, there will no longer be two religions in Arabia. I descended by Allah with the sword in my hand, and my wealth will come from the shadow of my sword. And the one who will disagree with me will be humiliated and persecuted."

A few months later, Muhammad fell ill and suffered for several days with head pain and weakness. He died in AD 634 at the age of sixty-three. He was buried in Aisha's house, which is now housed within the Mosque of the Prophet in Medina.

WATERSHED EVENTS

Now that we understand how Islam began and how Muhammad was able to convert most of the Arabian Peninsula to his new religion, we can begin to look at how Islam spread from there to the rest of the world and, ultimately, into American culture. To do so, however, we first need to discuss the concept of "watershed events," which are those significant situations that occur within a society or culture that change it forever. Sometimes, the participants in these watershed events do not recognize them as such when they occur, and it is only when they look back years later that they realize these events served as the spark that set the wheels of change in motion.

A few scenarios from the business world can provide us with some fairly recent examples of watershed events. For instance, thirty years ago in Mexico, it was possible to estimate the growth rate for the country's telephone company by analyzing how many phones there were for every one hundred people. You could see where the lines went and calculate how much time it would take for workers to put in poles and string the lines to reach new customers. However, all of these calculations were thrown off when cell phones were introduced. This represented a watershed event in the country's telecommunications and investment models.

We also see these events taking place in the retail industry. Ten years ago, if you wanted to purchase a book, you went to the bookstore. If you wanted to buy a CD, tape, or record, you went to the record store. Now a significant number of the population uses the Internet to make these purchases. Think of the competitive advantage this has given retailers such as Amazon. The company has no stores, hardly any employees, few mortgages, and can operate with little risk. It is a money machine. The growth of such retail outlets via the Internet has been a watershed event in the business world.

Going back further in history, we see that the invention of the automobile represented a watershed event. Prior to the mass production of the automobile in the early 1900s, trains had been the primary means of transportation. The people who owned the train companies had prospered, but this all changed when their passengers disappeared almost overnight. The automobile also helped end the days of the horse and buggy. In the late 1800s, the Fisher family owned a horse-drawn carriage shop in Norwalk, Ohio. In 1904, the two eldest brothers relocated to Detroit, Michigan, where they began adapting the body of the buggies for automobile manufacturers. (If you look at the panel inside the door of a GM car, you will see the words "Body by Fisher.") The company survived by adapting to the new era, but other companies that profited by selling buggy whips did not do the same, and most just disappeared.

Major moves in business and in world economics occur when there is secular change, and a watershed event often precedes this change. In a similar way, the foremost moves in cultures occur when there is a secular change. Again, such change is typically preceded or accompanied by a watershed event. Consider the effect that removing prayer and Bible reading from our public school system in the 1960s has had on the culture of the United States. Consider the negative changes that have occurred in our society as a result of removing this moral and spiritual base from our young people. This move represented a cultural watershed event.

THE RISE AND SPREAD OF ISLAM

The spread of Islam throughout the Middle East consisted of many watershed events. After Muhammad's death in AD 632, Abu Bakr, Muhammad's father-in-law and successor, initiated a number of successful campaigns against the waning Byzantine and Sassanian empires that dominated the Middle East. By AD 643, the Muslims had conquered all of Mesopotamia, Syria, Palestine, Egypt, and the entire Persian Empire. Many crusades and invasions have occurred since that time, with battles going back and forth. As a result, Islam has slowly spread, often through the sword, to every continent of the world.

To give you some historical perspective about Islam and the sword, it is interesting to note that between AD 1000 and 1500, invading Islamic armies killed at least sixty million Hindus in India.[3] This invasion included the systematic destruction of the local Hindu population, architecture, culture, and the enslavement of their women and children. As with other Islamic attacks against peoples of different religions, this was all done in accordance with the Muslim's most holy book, the Koran. This historical backdrop should provide those of us in the West with an understanding of why so much hatred still exists today between Hindus and Muslims in Pakistan and India. The two groups simply do not like each other, and the hostility between the two groups has existed for more than a thousand years.

During this time, the Ottoman Empire (1299–1923) rose to prominence in the Middle East. At its height, the empire spanned three continents and controlled much of southeastern Europe, western Asia, and northern Africa. Interestingly, it was the capture of an American ship in 1784 by the Ottoman state of Morocco in Africa that led to the creation of the United States Navy. From 1784 to 1800, the United States paid tribute to these "Barbary Pirates" to protect its ships in the region. America waged two successful wars against the Islamic empire from 1801 to 1815, which ultimately ended the payment of tribute.[4]

In preparation for these wars, Thomas Jefferson acquired a copy of the Koran to learn something about his enemy's religious and cultural beliefs.[5] Historian Robert C. Davis puts the number of Europeans enslaved for sale into Muslim lands from the sixteenth to nineteenth centuries at more than one million people. From 1914 to 1923, the Ottomans systematically killed approximately three million Armenians, Pontian Greeks, and Assyrians. This is widely acknowledged to have been one of the first modern genocides.[6]

ISLAM IN THE WEST

The relationship between Islam and the rest of the world remained a tug and pull until the invention of the internal combustion engine and the automobile in the late 1800s. As we have already seen, this was a watershed event that had a tremendous impact on the economy of the United States. However, it had implications that extended beyond the transportation industry.

After the dissolution of the Ottoman Empire at the end of World War I, the territories were divided into a number of independent nations. In 1932, Saudi Arabia became an independent country, and its territory encompassed Mecca, the holiest site of Islam. No one paid much attention to the Saudis until 1938, when another watershed event occurred: oil was discovered in Saudi Arabia and throughout the Middle East. The Muslim nations in these lands now possessed a resource the West greatly needed for its transportation industry. Slowly, the tide began to turn.

During World War II, Saudi Arabia played both sides of the fence until it became obvious that the Allies would win. Then in March 1945, just before the war came to an end, this nation declared war on Germany and Japan. After the war, development programs began in earnest and by 1949 oil production was in full effect. Since that time, oil has provided Saudi Arabia with economic prosperity and an enormous amount of political leverage. With Islam, we have secular change and cultural change occurring at the same time because of the vast amount of money coming into Muslim nations from the oil industry.

One of the benefits this has granted Saudi Arabia is the ability to invest in programs to promote Islam in non-Muslim nations. During the past two decades, the country has made available a documented $87 billion for Islamic missions in the Western hemisphere. In effect, the Saudis are using the money Americans pay them for oil to defeat and change their culture. Note that the actual sum of the money the Saudis invest is allegedly many times more than $87 billion when one includes the many terrorist organizations they sponsor. Remember that almost all of the 9/11 terrorists were state-sponsored Saudi nationals. Likewise, before the Gulf War, the Islamic nation of Kuwait budgeted $25 billion to blanket North America with Islamic propaganda.

Today, the practitioners of Islam are convinced that Allah has given them the victory because they have the oil, they have the money from the oil, and they have the power that it buys.

FOR STUDY AND REFLECTION

Consider the following questions based on the material you read in this chapter:

1. What medical problem do many scholars believe Muhammad had? How did this condition lead to some of the revelations he claimed?

2. Why did Khadija, Muhammad's wife at the time, go along with his claim to be a prophet? What did she do next?

3. Why did the Jews reject Muhammad's claim that he was the greatest prophet who ever lived? Why did the Christians also reject his claim?

4. What occupation did Muhammad assume after the death of his first wife? How did this aid him in spreading Islam?

5. Why was Muhammad's new religion appealing to most of the men in Arabia?

6. What are some of the "watershed events" that led to the growth of Islam in the world?

To conclude this chapter, I suggest you view the first ten minutes of *Jihad in America* after the introduction. Again, you can find the video online at youtube.com or on Google videos at http://video.google.com/videoplay?docid =-9172967809538239506#. Stop the video after the interview with Paul Bremer, ambassador-at-large for counterterrorism in the U.S. State Department during the 1980s.

After reviewing the clip, answer the following questions:

1. Anwar Sadat, "President" of Egypt, was a Muslim. Why did other Muslims assassinate him?

2. Whom do the terrorists say controls the world?

3. According to the video, what is the goal of jihad?

4. What became of the Islamic fighters whom the United States helped in Afghanistan during the fight against communism in the 1980s?

5. Do you agree or disagree with Paul Bremer's statement that the fight against terrorism is not a fight against Islam? Would you say it is a fight against Arabs? Against both Islam and the Arabs? Against neither Islam nor the Arabs?

It is interesting to note that Mr. Sadat was forced into negotiations with Israel due to geopolitical events. This interchange was not something he would have freely chosen. This is somewhat ironic, as the fact that he engaged in such meetings is often put forth as a driving reason for why he was assassinated.

During the negotiations with Israel and when meeting with the Israeli Knesset, Sadat wore a tie emblazoned with large swastikas. Manachem Begin, the Israeli Prime Minister at the time, was heard to remark, "I didn't like his tie, and I didn't like his letter." The letter to which Mr. Begin refers is as follows:

His Excellency Jimmy Carter
President of the United States

September 17, 1978

Dear Mr. President:

I am writing you to reaffirm the position of the Arab Republic of Egypt with respect to Jerusalem:

1. Arab Jerusalem is an integral part of the West Bank. Legal and historical Arab rights in the City must be respected and restored.
2. Arab Jerusalem should be under Arab sovereignty.
3. The Palestinian inhabitants of Arab Jerusalem are entitled to exercise their legitimate national rights, being part of the Palestinian People in the West Bank.
4. Relevant Security Council Resolutions, particularly Resolutions 242 and 267, must be applied with regard to Jerusalem. All the measures taken by Israel to alter the status of the City are null and void and should be rescinded.
5. All peoples must have free access to the City and enjoy the free exercise of worship and the right to visit and transit to the holy places without distinction or discrimination.
6. The holy places of each faith may be placed under the administration and control of their representatives.
7. Essential functions in the City should be undivided, and a joint municipal council composed of an equal number of Arab and Israeli members can supervise the carrying out of these functions. In this way, the city shall be undivided.

Sincerely,

Mohammed Anwar El Sadat[7]

Manachem Begin also wrote to Jimmy Carter about the same issue. His letter is as follows:

Prime Minister's Bureau

The President
Camp David
Thurmont, Maryland

17 September, 1978

Dear Mr. President:

I have the honor to inform you, Mr. President, that on 28 June, 1967—Israel's Parliament (The Knesset) promulgated and adopted a law to the effect: "The Government is empowered by a decree to apply the law, the jurisdiction, and administration of the State to any part of Eretz Israel (land of Israel—Palestine), as stated in that decree."

On the basis of this Law, the Government of Israel decreed in July 1967 that Jerusalem is one city, indivisible, the Capital of the State of Israel.

Sincerely,

Manachem Begin[8]

From these letters, you can see uncomfortable and diametrically opposed positions of the Muslims and Israelis during that time.

CHAPTER FOUR
TENETS AND CUSTOMS OF ISLAM

NOW THAT WE have examined how Islam was founded and how it spread throughout the world, we need to spend some time examining some of the primary tenets of the religion and the customs that Muslims are required to practice. As we begin this study, keep in mind that when Muhammad was creating his religion, he cobbled together bits and pieces of other religions and cultural practices he had heard about from traveling merchants who passed through Mecca. If he came across something from a religious or political system that he thought he could use to his advantage, he incorporated it into his religion.

ARTICLES OF FAITH

Muslims believe in a god they call "Allah." They presume this deity to be the same God as the God of the Jews and the Christians, but in fact Allah is very different. In the Koran, Allah is described as follows: "Say: He is God, the One and Only; God, the Eternal, Absolute; He begetteth not, nor is He begotten; and there is none like unto Him" (Sura 112:1-4). Like the God of the Bible, Allah is given certain names that supposedly refer to his attributes, such as *Al-Rahman* ("the compassionate," "the beneficent," or "the gracious"), *Al-Rahim* ("the merciful") and *Al-Salam* ("the peace and blessing"), although he is clearly none of these.

As previously stated, the word "Muslim" literally means "one who gives himself to God," and it denotes a follower of Islam. Muslims try to confuse people by claiming that Jesus, Moses, Abraham, and other persons in the Bible who adhered to a monotheistic belief system (the belief that there is only one God) were Muslims because of this literal meaning. Nothing could be further from the truth! The God of the Judeo-Christian Scriptures is diametrically opposed to the god of Muhammad. However, this provides a good example of Muslims' roundabout thinking and deceptive semantics.

Muslims also believe in angels who, much as in Judaism and Christianity, serve as messengers between Allah and humans. Angels are responsible for communicating revelations from Allah (much as Muhammad claimed the angel Gabriel did during his seizure in the cave at Hira), glorifying Allah, recording people's actions, and taking their souls when they die. In the Koran, they are visualized as "messengers with wings—two, or three, or four (pairs)" (Sura 35:1).

In addition to angels and humans, Islam teaches that Allah created another class of sentient beings called the *jinn* (or genies). The *jinn* are supernatural beings who are made of smokeless flame or "the fire of a scorching wind" (Sura 15:27), and they have the ability to change their shape. Unlike the demonic forces depicted in the Bible, the *jinn* can be good, evil, or neutral. It is interesting to note that the *jinn* existed in the myths of many Middle Eastern cultures before the time of Muhammad. Ancient inscriptions found in northwestern Arabia seem to indicate that the pagan peoples worshiped the *jinn,* describing them as "the good and rewarding gods." Muhammad, when stating he was sent as a prophet to both "humanity and the jinn," simply adapted these local myths and folklores into his new religion.

The most holy book in Islam is the Koran, which Muslims view as the final revelation of Allah and his literal word. As we have already discussed, Muhammad claimed that the angel Gabriel delivered the first verses of the Koran to him during his episodes in the cave at Hira in AD 610. He claimed the angel continued delivering the verses until the time of his death in AD 632. Muhammad believed that portions of the previously revealed Scriptures—what we call the Bible—had become distorted in some way, which is why he claimed that Allah had sent the angel to him. In a later chapter, we will examine some of the theories of how the

Koran was recorded (remember that Muhammad was illiterate), some of the many inaccuracies in it, and why the Bible is the only true and infallible revelation of God to His people.

As might be expected, prophets also play a key role in Islam. The Koran mentions many names of individuals in the Bible whom they consider to be prophets, including Adam, Noah, Abraham, Ishmael, and Jesus (note that while they deny Jesus is the Son of God, they do allow Him to be a prophet). Ishmael, as you may recall, was the son of Abraham and Hagar, Sarah's handmaiden, whom Abraham sent away after conflict arose between Hagar and Sarah (see Genesis 16). According to Islamic tradition, Adam first built the Ka'aba, and then Abraham and Ishmael rebuilt the structure on the old foundations (see Sura 2:127). Muhammad reserved the role of the greatest prophet for himself, claiming that he had been sent by Allah to basically "sum up" what all of these other prophets had been saying and correctly interpret the will of Allah to mankind.

Muslims believe in a great Judgment Day. On that day, they believe Allah will tally up all of their good works and decide their fate (unless they die in *jihad,* at which point they will receive their reward automatically). As we have mentioned, the Islamic idea of heaven is basically "an enormous God-owned bordello in the sky,"[1] where Muslim men get to have their sexual desires fulfilled by scores of virgins. The great Judgment Day is also the time at which the Dar al Harb will be annihilated and the Dar Al Islam will prevail.

THE FIVE PILLARS OF ISLAM

When Muhammad established his new religion, he set out five basic acts or "pillars" that he deemed obligatory for his followers to practice. At first glance, these pillars seem innocuous enough, until one realizes their implications and the fullness of the associated belief system.

Pillar 1: The Statement of Belief

All those who wish to follow Islam must accept the Muslim statement of faith known as the Shahadah: "There is no god but Allah, and Muhammad is his prophet." In this prayer, the person basically confirms his or her faith in Allah and his or her full obedience to the commands of Allah as revealed to Muhammad. (This was the prayer the seventh-graders in California were told to recite as part of their course in Islam.) This pillar is foundational to all of the other beliefs and practices in Islam, and Muslims are required to repeat it frequently.

Pillar 2: Ritual Prayer

Muslims must pray five times a day while facing Mecca, the birthplace of Muhammad. Prayers are said at dawn, afternoon, late afternoon, after sunset, and at night. The ritualized daily prayers are called Salat, Salaat, Salah, or Salah, depending on who is doing the spelling (it appears that all are acceptable). One of the regular sessions performed each day is replaced by a special service on Fridays.

The Hadith tells a story that explains why Muslims must pray exactly five times each day. The claim is that Muhammad was riding on a donkey that could fly, and he flew up to paradise to talk with Allah. There, Allah instructed him to tell the Muslims to pray and bow toward Mecca fifty times each day. Muhammad said that he would do so, and he flew down to talk to Moses about it.

When Moses heard the number, he told Muhammad that it was too many times. He instructed him to go back and talk to Allah about it, so Muhammad flew back up to paradise and reported what Moses had said. Allah agreed that it was too many times and said that forty times would be all right. So Muhammad flew back down on his winged donkey to talk to Moses again. Moses said forty times was still too many and that Muhammad needed a better discount.

Once again, Muhammad flew back up to talk to Allah. This went on continuously. Muhammad flew up and down until Allah finally agreed on a number of five times each day to pray. Moses agreed with that number. Of course, this story neglects the fact that Moses was dead long before Muhammad lived. It also neglects the fact that donkeys can't fly. It does provide evidence, however, of the influence the bartering tradition has had in the Arabian culture. We will examine some other beliefs, rituals, and customs associated with these ritual prayers in the following section.

Pillar 3: Giving Alms

Muslims are required to give a fixed portion of their wealth through almsgiving (*zakat*). This is similar to paying a tax, and it must be paid by the end of the year. Remember from the last chapter that giving alms was the tax Muhammad imposed on the tribes that surrendered to him. Muslims are still required to give alms today to "those in need." This category of individuals can include those who need food and shelter, but it can also include those who need ammunition and bombs to kill members of the Dar Al Harb, which—as you might recall—includes anyone reading this book who is not a Muslim.

Pillar 4: Fasting

All Muslims must partake in a special fast (*sawm*) during the Islamic month of Ramadan. According to the Islamic calendar, this fast begins at the first visual sighting of the ninth crescent moon. During Ramadan, Muslims eat a light meal (and drink a lot of water) before daybreak, and then do not eat or drink anything else during the daylight hours. After the sun sets, they eat a heavier meal and again consume a lot of liquid.

The month of Ramadan is significant in Islamic culture because it was supposedly the time when Allah gave Muhammad the Koran during his epileptic fits. The practitioners of other religions in the area were already fasting during this month, so Muhammad just took over the tradition. However, he couldn't afford to have his bandits fast for a full month. If they did, they would not have had the strength to fight off their enemies and pillage caravans.

So Muhammad figured out a way to get around the regulation. He had his men get up early and enjoy a hearty breakfast, and then he sent them out to fight, pillage, kill, enslave, and rape. He made certain they finished a little early so they could get back for the evening feast. All they really had to do was skip lunch.

Pillar 5: Pilgrimage

All able-bodied Muslims who can afford to do so are required to make a pilgrimage to Mecca, called a *haj* or *hajj*, at least once during their lifetime. The pilgrimage occurs from the eighth to twelfth day of Dhu al-Hijjah, which is the last month of the Islamic calendar. When the pilgrims reach Mecca, they participate in a five-day ritual that includes (1) walking counterclockwise seven times around the Ka'aba, (2) going back and forth between the hills of Al-Safa and Al-Marwah, (3) drinking from the sacred Zamzam well, (4) travelling to the plains of Mount Arafat and standing in vigil, and (5) throwing stones in a ritual act.[2]

This is yet another example of how Muhammad piggybacked on existing customs. The tribes in the region were already traveling on pilgrimages to Mecca to visit their idols at the Ka'aba, kiss the big black stone, and throw rocks off the mountain where Muhammad was allegedly born. You might recall that Muhammad's tribe ran the concession for these events, as they were the ones who took care of the Ka'aba. All the pilgrims left offerings of food, money, or goods for their idols, which Muhammad's tribe kept for themselves. He just continued the tradition for his benefit when he established his rule and religion.

MUSLIM PRAYERS AND RITUAL MOTIONS

Before Muslims say their daily ritualized prayers, they must engage in *wudu*, which is a form of ritual ambulation that involves washing the hands, teeth, nose, arms, hair, ears, and feet three times in a row in proper order. If no water is available, it is acceptable for the practitioner to use sand. Note that Muslims do not necessarily have to do this ritual each time—if they used water earlier in the day and do not believe they have "sinned" (according to their definition), they do not have to wash before the next prayer. If they wash with sand for one prayer, they must again wash with sand or water before the next prayer.

As part of the daily prayers, Muslims must go through ritual motions called *rakat, raka,* or *raka'ah*. One particular *rakat* involves (1) kneeling, (2) standing, (3) sitting on one's knees, (4) placing one's face and hands on a prayer rug, (5) sitting up, (6) placing one's face and hands on the prayer rug again, and (7) sitting up. These *rakat* rituals are performed at each time of prayer. After the *rakat* is complete, the worshiper recites the first Sura from the Koran and follows this by repeatedly reciting certain key concepts and phrases. An example of this is as follows:

Allah Akbar.

Muhammad is the Messenger of Allah.

Come to prayer.

Allah Akbar.

There is none worthy of worship except Allah.

Allah Akbar.

The first Sura of the Koran, which the worshipers must recite (the *fatiha*), is often referred to as the "Muslim Lord's Prayer." The passage is as follows:

In the name of Allah, the Beneficent, the Merciful. All praise is due because of Allah, the Lord of the Worlds. The Beneficent. The Merciful. Master of the Day of Judgment. Thee only do we serve and Thee only do we beseech for help. Keep us on the right path. The path of those upon whom thou hast bestowed favors. Not the path of those upon whom Thy wrath is brought down, nor of those who go astray.

—Sura 1:1-7

Note the similarities between this prayer and the Lord's Prayer in the Judeo-Christian Scriptures:

After this manner therefore pray ye: Our Father which art in heaven, Hallowed be thy name. Thy kingdom come. Thy will be done in earth, as it is in heaven. Give us this day our daily bread. And forgive us our debts, as we forgive our debtors. And lead us not into temptation, but deliver us from evil: For thine is the kingdom, and the power, and the glory, for ever. Amen.

—Matthew 6:9-13 KJV

Like Muhammad's Sermon on Mount Ararat, this is just another counterfeit in Islam copied directly from the Christian Bible. As we continue our study, you will see that there are many such counterfeits. Also, it is important to keep in mind that more is implied in the "Muslim Lord's Prayer" than appears on the surface. In a later chapter, we will examine who Allah is, the kind of help the worshipers are asking Allah to provide, and how Muslims are directed to punish "those who go astray."

There is one final, crowning blow to consider regarding these Islamic prayer rituals: they are always recited in Arabic. The problem is that most Muslims in the world cannot read or speak Arabic. They may learn to recite phrases in the language, *but they have absolutely no idea what they are saying.*

PRAYER RUGS

While Muslims are not required to kneel on rugs during their prayers and ritual motions, they are required to use a clean area for praying. For this reason, the use of prayer rugs has become a traditional way of ensuring the cleanliness of the place in which they are praying. After the Muslims' time of bowing, kneeling, and prostration is over, they immediately fold or roll up the rug and put it away until the next use. Poorer Muslims use rush mats and sometimes newspapers if they cannot afford a rug.

The rugs themselves often have symbols of a mosque on them so the worshipers can feel that their mosque is always with them. The rugs are decorated with a prayer niche, called a *mihrab* or *qibla*, which is a concept of Islamic architecture where a niche is placed in the wall of a mosque closest to Mecca. The worshipers point the niche on the rug toward Mecca when they lay it out for prayer. One of my Christian friends from an Islamic country is often asked the direction of Mecca because of his obvious ethnicity. He delights in the inside joke of pointing worshipers in the wrong direction to pray. This, of course, means that the part of the worshiper's body opposite his head is pointing toward Mecca.

The Arabic word for a prayer rug is *sajada*, which comes from the same root word as *masjed* (mosque) and *sujud* (prostration). Strangely, this definition leads us to the legend of the magic carpet. Islamic tradition dictates that Solomon "had a carpet of green silk, on which his throne was placed, being of a prodigious length and breadth, and sufficient for all his forces to stand on, the men pacing themselves on his right hand, and the spirits on his left; and that when all were in order, the wind, at his command, took up the carpet and transported it, with all that were upon it, wherever he pleased; the army of birds at the same time flying over their heads, and forming a kind of canopy, to shade them from the sun."[3] The spirits mentioned in this passage are the *jinn*, or genies, who are often interwoven with tales of flying carpets. Muslims state that this tradition refers to Sura 38:33-35 and Sura 27:20-26, 38-40, though the flying carpet is not mentioned in the Koran.

SPECIAL WORSHIP SERVICES

During the special worship services on Friday, Muslims are treated to a comparison between Jesus and Muhammad and a harangue against the "People of the Book." In more fundamental Islamic societies, this worship service also includes special ceremonies such as the beheadings of Muslims caught in adultery or fornication during the week or the removal of people's hands who were caught stealing. The Islamic members carry out other executions and physical punishments as are deemed appropriate. The more fundamental the country, the more cruelly they carry out their traditions.

It is difficult to obtain reliable statistics about these practices in closed societies. In one limited and partial report, Amnesty International stated that in 2000 there were 123 such executions in Saudi Arabia. The body of one of those put to death, an Egyptian national, was crucified following his execution. The report also cited thirty-four cases of amputation, seven of which were cross-amputations (of the right hand and left foot). Another Egyptian national had his left eye surgically removed as a punishment handed down by a court in Medina, and two teachers arrested during demonstrations in Najran were sentenced to 15,000 lashes each in front of their families, students, and other teachers. If you know anything about whips, you will realize that 15,000 lashes is a sentence of a gradual, brutal, bloody, and painful death. Torturing prisoners, including electric shock, is common in such Muslim societies.[4]

It is interesting to note that when the Disney film *Aladdin* was released in 1992, it drew protests from Islamic groups, who objected to the opening character singing about how he came from a land in a faraway place "where they cut off your ear if they don't like your face." These groups took great umbrage at this accurate depiction of life in radical Islamic culture and convinced Disney to change the line. In the 1993 video release (and subsequent rereleases), the character now sings, "where it's flat and immense and the heat is intense."

ISLAMIC LAW

One final custom in Islam is *sharia* (literally "the path leading to the watering place"), which is Islamic law formed by Islamic scholarship. *Sharia* deals with many aspects of secular law, such as crime, politics, and economics, but it also deals with issues of daily living, such as sexuality, hygiene, diet, prayer, and fasting. In Muslim countries where *sharia* has official status, it is applied to cases by Islamic judges, or *qadis*. The punishments for these offenses, as we have discussed in the previous section, are often severe.

Recently, the British newspapers *The Sunday Times* and the *Daily Mail* reported on a little-known clause in the United Kingdom's legal system that allows *sharia* courts to issue some civil and criminal verdicts that are legally binding. The country's Arbitration Act of 1996 states that the *sharia* courts qualify as tribunals, and that their rulings are enforceable by county and high courts when both sides agree to use the tribunal to settle a dispute. *Sharia* courts are already operating in five major British cities and have handed down binding rulings on divorce, financial disputes, and domestic violence. This sobering and frightening situation will become even more alarming when we discuss the place of women in Islam in a later chapter.

FOR STUDY AND REFLECTION

Consider the following questions based on the material you read in this chapter:

1. What are the functions and purpose of angels in Islam? What are the *jinn*? In what ways are the *jinn* similar to angels? In what ways are they different?

2. Why did Muhammad claim that Allah had sent the angel Gabriel to him? What supposed error was he correcting?

3. How do Muslims view the afterlife? What do Muslims believe will happen on Judgment Day?

4. What are the five pillars of Islam?

5. What are some of the rituals associated with prayer in Islam?

6. What occurs in some of the fundamental Islamic nations during the special worship services on Fridays? Why is it difficult to get accurate statistics about the number of people this involves?

7. As we have mentioned during this study, Jews and Christians are in the same boat as far as Muslims are concerned. Muslims lump these two groups together and refer to them as "The People of the Book." In fact, Jews and Christians do share many things in common. List ten commonalities between the two faiths:

   1.

   2.

   3.

   4.

   5.

   6.

7.

8.

9.

10.

If you are stuck, here are ten commonalities I have found between Christians and Jews:

1. Both believe in a Jewish Messiah who speaks Hebrew.
2. Both worship from a Jewish Bible. (Most Jews do not realize that the New Testament, like the Old Testament, is a Jewish book; many Christians fail to recognize their Jewish roots.)
3. Both were founded by Jewish leadership.
4. Both derive the benefits they have from the covenant God established with Abraham.
5. Both believe in the coming or return of a Jewish Messiah who speaks Hebrew.
6. Both believe in the one true God as revealed in Judeo-Christian Scriptures.
7. Both believe in the Old Testament as the inerrant Word of God. (Messianic Jews recognize that this also extends to the New Testament, and that the Bible is one book comprised of sixty-six cohesive books.)
8. Both believe in the same basic concepts of righteousness, prayer, and the afterlife.
9. Both believe in the same system of conduct, life, and action as revealed in Judeo-Christian Scriptures.
10. Both believe Genesis 12:3, in which God says to the Jews, "I will bless those who bless you and curse those who curse you. All the families of the earth will be blessed through you" (NLT).

In the remaining chapters of this book, we will examine some of the inter-relationships between the roots of Judaism and Christianity and compare the God of the Bible with the god of Islam. We will also look at the Muslim claim that the Koran is the divine word of God and that Islam is a religion of peace and love. In delving into these issues and examining what Islam really says, we will expose many errors and inaccuracies and reveal how these claims are simply not true. As we begin this portion of the study, ask God for clearer understanding of His Word and pray for the Muslims who are caught in this web of deception.

CHAPTER FIVE

THE KORAN AND THE BIBLE

AS WE HAVE seen, Muslims believe that the Koran was revealed to Muhammad throughout his life by the angel Gabriel. Muslims hold that the Koran is the divine word of Allah given through his principal prophet, Muhammad, and that it is Allah's *final* revelation to his people. To Muslims, the Koran offers the sum total of Allah's guidance and moral direction for mankind. (Realize here that the emphasis is on *man*kind—from the beginning women have never been very welcome in the religion.)

In this regard, many Muslims will state that they accept the Judeo-Christian Scriptures. However, a reading of both will show that such a claim is built on either wishful thinking or unfortunate ignorance about the documents themselves and what they actually have to say. In addition, when Muslims say they accept the Bible, they do so with the caveat that the Koran is the divine and infallible word of Muhammad and that it replaces the Bible.

HOW THE KORAN WAS WRITTEN

The fact that Muhammad was illiterate has caused many people to question exactly how the Koran was first recorded. Many Muslims believe that the writing of the Koran represented a miracle—the miracle of an illiterate man being able to compose text—despite the fact that Muhammad spoke against miracles and said that he could not perform any (see Sura 2:118; 2:145; 6:37; 6:109; 10:20; 17:59). Also, as stated in the Koran, Muhammad's function was to "warn" people, not to perform miracles (see Sura 13:7).

Some modern Muslim scholars believe that the Koran was written down later by a caliph who simply organized notes left by Muhammad. Exactly *how* an illiterate man could leave notes is up for debate, and given the fact that the Koran is about six hundred pages long, it would mean that he would have had to leave a lot of notes behind. Given this, it seems it would have been easier to just *write* the Koran and save the trouble of taking down all those notes.

One of the more credible theories of how the Koran was written comes from examining the language in the text and the historical situation at the time it was written. In the ancient world, if you were illiterate and you wanted to communicate to someone in a different village, you would hire a scribe to write a message for you. During Muhammad's time, the best scribes came from a religious Jewish background. They were trained to be meticulous, and they made very few mistakes in their writing. Given Muhammad's profession as a bandit, it is likely that he and his followers kidnapped a scribe (or scribes) and had them write down the Koran.

One of these theories states that the Muslims kidnapped a Jewish rabbi and an Armenian or Syrian priest, put them in a pit, and promised they would be set free when they finished writing the book. According to this theory, Muhammad himself dictated what he wanted them to write. The men performed their task, and—in character with the theology of Islam—they were killed when they finished their work. If this story is true, it would have given the Jewish rabbi and the priest tremendous liberty to put things in the text that the Muslims would not have known about, as they could not read the text to verify what it said.

This leads to an interesting discovery. Hebrew is a complex language, with an alphanumeric structure. This means that the letters and words all have numerical values and meaning. Because of this, it is possible to encode messages into the text below the surface. These messages would only be detectable by someone familiar with the Hebrew language.

When we look at the Koran, we find that when it is translated into Hebrew there are two alphanumeric messages hidden in the text. No one in the Islamic world knows how to decode these messages, as they do not understand the alphanumeric linguistic used by Jewish rabbis. The two messages incorporated into the linguistic structure can be translated to mean, "These verses mean nothing" or "I don't believe any of this." This type of "correction" is what you would expect a Jewish rabbi and a priest to sneak into the text if they were being forced to write a book like the Koran.

HISTORICAL ERRORS AND FOLKLORE

If the Koran were the divine word of God, it would stand to reason that it would not contain any errors. However, when we examine the book, we find that many of the stories do not add up to the facts as revealed through history. Here is a summary of only a few of the errors:

1. Sura 7:51 and 10:3 claim that there were six days of creation, while Sura 41 claims that there were eight days. Genesis 1 states that God created the universe in six days and then rested on the seventh day.
2. Sura 7:59 and 7:136 state that the Great Flood occurred during the days of Moses. Genesis 6–9 shows that the flood occurred during the time of Noah.
3. Sura 6:74 states that Abraham's father was named Azar. Genesis 11:27 states that his name was Terah.
4. Sura 14:37 states that Abraham lived in Mecca. Genesis 11:31 states that Abraham was originally from Ur of the Chaldeans before he travelled to Canaan.
5. Sura 37:100-112 states that Abraham had only two sons. Genesis 25 states that Abraham had taken another wife, who bore him other sons.
6. Muslims today claim that Abraham took his son Ishmael to be sacrificed. (Note that the Koran does not say this—Muslims *added* it because the Koran does not mention which son it was. Muslims believe that if Abraham was going to sacrifice his son, it must have been Ishmael. However, this directly

contradicts all historical documents, including Genesis 22, which states that the son was Isaac.)

7. Muslims also claim that Nimrod threw Abraham into a fiery furnace, or at least that Nimrod dreamed about it. There is no proof of this. Daniel 3 tells a story that is historically accurate.

8. Sura 85:21-22 states that the Koran is free from error.

Archaeological and linguistic work conducted since the latter part of the nineteenth century has uncovered overwhelming evidence that Muhammad built much of his religion and the text of the Koran from existing material in the Arabian culture. Here are just a few examples of Muhammad's borrowings:

1. Sura 18:60-65 tells the story of "Moses and the Fish," which comes from Arabic folktales about the search for eternal life. It is possible that this legend originated in Babylon, as there is a similar story in Babylonian myth about the god El.

2. Sura 27:15-19 relates a story about King Solomon speaking with ants, which was a fairy tale, perhaps inspired by Proverbs 6:6. The story in the Koran also states that *jinns* worked in the service of Solomon. *Jinns*, or genies, were fixtures in local folklore at the time of Muhammad.

3. Sura 19:29-33 tells how the infant Jesus spoke from the crib. This was taken from the religious legend "The Egyptian Child Gospel." Other stories in the Koran relating miraculous things the infant Jesus did are taken from other Gnostic texts.

4. Sura 18:9-26 relates a story about youths who took refuge in a cave and miraculously woke up 300 or 309 years later. This is actually based on a well-known fable from Ephesus about seven youths who fled from the persecutions under the Emperor Decius (AD 201–251), fell asleep in a cave, and woke up around 190 years later. There is even a Cave of the Seven Sleepers in Turkey.

5. Sura 18:89-98 speaks of a man named Dhul-Qarnayn, which literally translates as "Two-Horned," a common title of Alexander the Great in the

Middle East during the time of Muhammad. The story appears to be taken from the "Romance of Alexander," a narrative that transforms Alexander the Great into a monotheist.

It is interesting to note that the versions of the Koran printed in this country change constantly. Many versions are being systematically sanitized to read in a way that will agree with uninformed readers. These "versions" are not true to Islam and are deceptive. Generally, the more recent the version, the more sanitized it is. If you want to prove this to yourself, go to a good bookstore that stocks ten or so translations of the Koran. Note the dates of translation and the publication and then compare a few of the key Suras. You will likely be amazed.

Perhaps you remember the old television series *Mission Impossible,* which aired in the late 1960s. Most episodes began with the secret agents receiving orders about their next mission from a hidden tape recorder and an envelope of photos and information. The voice on the tape explained the mission and then said, "This tape will self-destruct in five seconds. Good luck." This is just like the Koran. The more you read the book, the more it self-destructs.

When all is said and done, the Koran is nothing more than a compilation of stories and sayings from Hinduism, Buddhism, Mysticism, Greek mythology, Judaism, Christianity, and Arabic folklore. As such, it is confused and contradictory throughout.

MUHAMMAD'S (MISSING) SOURCES

At this point you may well be asking yourself, *How did this happen? How could Muhammad get so many of the stories wrong?* To answer these questions, you have to remember that Muhammad led a caravan before he married into wealth. During his caravan years, he traveled extensively and interacted with people from various cultures and religions.[1] When he cobbled his religion together, he included what he could remember from these sources—regardless of whether or not it was accurate.

The Bible was not available in Arabic until two hundred years after the death of Muhammad, around AD 824, so Muhammad could not refer to it. (Of course, if it had been available during Muhammad's time, it would not have done him any good anyway, since he could not read or write.) Muhammad had to take the stories that he had picked up on his travels and incorporate them into the Koran from memory. In most instances, he either remembered the stories incorrectly or received bad information.

Muslim scholars are willing to admit that parts of the original Koran were lost and that subsequent scholars tried to reconstruct them. We know from history that the caliph Abu Baker (AD 573–634) collected the different chapters and verses of the Koran into one volume after Muhammad's death. Around AD 650, the caliph Uthman ibn Affan ordered the creation of an "official" and standardized version. Five scholars produced a unique text from the first volume, and the other copies in the hands of Muslims in other areas were collected and destroyed.

However, according to a report by the son of the caliph Umar ibn al-Khattab, much of the text of that version of the Koran was incomplete: "Abdullah b. 'Umar reportedly said, 'Let none of you say, "I have got the whole of the Qu'ran." How does he know what all of it is? Much of the Qu'ran has gone. Let him say instead, "I have got what has survived."'"[2] Ibn Hazm, an Islamic scholar, reveals how some of the pages were lost: "The verses of stoning and breast-feeding were in the possession of A'isha in a Qur'anic copy. When Muhammad died and people became busy in the burial preparations, a domesticated animal entered and ate it."[3] Despite this, the typical Muslim today regards the Koran as the divine, infallible word of Allah as revealed to his prophet Muhammad.

THE HADITH

Besides the Koran, Muslims have other sacred books and writings, including the Hadith, which are claimed to be narrations concerning something Muhammad did or taught. Muslims themselves struggle with some of the contradictions found in the Hadith and choose what they want to believe from it. The difference between the Hadith and the Koran is that Muhammad was involved in writing the Koran directly. Again, his involvement was limited to allegedly dictating the text to writers, as he was unable to read or write.

EXAMINING THE JUDEO-CHRISTIAN SCRIPTURES

In the remainder of this chapter, we will turn our attention to the Judeo-Christian Scriptures. We will first look at what the Bible says about itself and then examine the historical accuracy of this document. In doing so, we will follow the model of the Berean Jews, who "received the word with all readiness, and searched the Scriptures daily to find out whether these things were so" (Acts 17:11 NKJV). As you read the information in this section, I ask you to test what you learn here (and elsewhere) against this standard to determine for yourself whether the Bible is truly the only undeniable and irrefutable Word of God.

Scripture Is Inspired

The first item we need to consider is what the Bible says about itself. In this regard, we find several places in both the Old and New Testaments where the biblical writers attest to the *authority* and *inspiration* of the Judeo-Christian Scriptures. The apostle Paul states this clearly in 2 Timothy 3:16-17 when he writes, "All scripture is inspired by God and is useful for teaching the truth, rebuking error, correcting fault and giving instruction for right living so the man who serves God may be fully qualified and equipped for every kind of good work" (GNT).

In this passage, Paul states that Scripture is vital for teaching the truth and correcting fault. In 1 Thessalonians 5:21-22, he explains that we should "test everything that is said by the standard of Scripture . . . test everything that is said. Hold on to what is good. Keep away from every kind of evil" (NLT). Jesus likewise taught that every detail of the Tanakh and the New Testament has meaning and that it was written for a purpose. In Matthew 5:17-18, He states, "Do not think that I came to destroy the Law or the Prophets. I did not come to destroy but to fulfill. For assuredly, I say to you, till heaven and earth pass away, one jot or one tittle will by no means pass from the law till all is fulfilled" (NKJV).

Unlike the Koran, which Muslims claim was revealed to one man through a revelation from the angel Gabriel, God inspired many ordinary men to write the message He wanted to communicate to His creation. "For prophecy never came by the will of man, but holy men of God spoke as they were moved by the Holy

Spirit" (2 Peter 1:21). Scripture is inspired because *God inspired it,* and He will fulfill what He has said in His Word. Furthermore, Psalm 138:2 tells us that God values this inspired Word even above His name: "I will worship toward thy holy temple, and praise thy name for thy lovingkindness and for thy truth: for thou hast magnified thy word above all thy name" (KJV).

Scripture Is Complete

One of the reasons Muhammad gave for writing the Koran was that the Tanakh and New Testament did not represent the complete word of God and needed an "addition" to capture His final and perfect revelation. However, as we see from the biblical writers, nothing could be further from the truth. As far back as the time of the Exodus, leaders such as Moses were warning the people, "Do not add or take away from His Word. See that you do all I command you; do not add to it or take away from it" (NLT).

We see this stated even more clearly in Proverbs 30:5-6: "Every word of God is flawless; he is a shield to those who take refuge in him. Do not add to his words, or he will rebuke you and prove you a liar" (NIV). Indeed, this is what we have seen has happened in Muhammad's case. Furthermore, the prophet Jeremiah warns not to attempt to diminish or reduce God's inspired Word: "Thus saith Jehovah: 'Stand in the court of Jehovah's house, and speak unto all the cities of Judah, which come to worship in Jehovah's house, all the words that I command thee to speak unto them; diminish not a word'" (ASV).

In the New Testament, we see that Paul also warned people not to attempt to alter the Word of God: "If we, *or an angel from heaven*, preach any other gospel to you than what we have preached to you, let him be accursed. As we have said before, so now I say again, if anyone preaches any other gospel to you than what you have received, let him be accursed" (Gal. 1:8-9 NKJV, emphasis added). It is ironic that this is exactly what Muhammad claimed—that the angel Gabriel had revealed this "new" gospel to him. Perhaps if he had heard these final words from John, he might have considered his actions more carefully: "I warn everyone who hears the words of the prophecy of this scroll: If anyone adds anything to them, God will add to that person the plagues described in this scroll. And if anyone takes words away from this scroll of prophecy, God will take away from that person any share in the tree of life and in the Holy City, which are described in this scroll" (Rev. 22:18-19 NIV).

Scripture Produces Fruit

One of the best ways to determine if anything is truly from God is to see if it produces fruit in a person's life. In Isaiah 55:11, the prophet makes this claim: God's word does not return to him void. "It is the same with my word. I send it out, and it always produces fruit. It will accomplish all I want it to, and it will prosper everywhere I send it" (NLT). Time and again, we have seen the truth of these words. Wherever the gospel of Christ goes—whatever nation or group of people in the world it reaches—it brings transformation and change for the better among the population. As Paul wrote, "Christ loved the church and gave himself up for her to make her holy, cleansing her by the washing with water through the word, and to present her to himself as a radiant church, without stain or wrinkle or any other blemish, but holy and blameless" (Eph. 5:25-27 NIV).

Scripture Is Eternal

A final point to note about Scripture is that it is eternal. In Isaiah 40:8, the prophet writes, "His Word will stand forever. The grass withers, and the flowers fade, but the word of our God stands forever" (NLT). In Psalm 111:7-8, the author states, "The works of [God's] hands are truth and justice; all His precepts are sure. They are upheld forever and ever; they are performed in truth and uprightness" (NASB). Jesus also affirmed this truth in Matthew 24:35: "Heaven and earth will disappear, but my words will remain forever" (NLT). God's inspired Word will last forever. It will never go out of existence.

THE HISTORICAL ACCURACY OF THE BIBLE

When we refer to the Judeo-Christian Scriptures, what we actually have is a collection of sixty-six separate books by at least forty different authors from all different walks of life, written over a period of about 1,400 years. Yet despite this diversity in the Bible's construction, it is clear that every detail was placed there by design as part of an "integrated message system." This is because every book of the Bible carries the same unifying theme: God is the loving Creator who desires to redeem fallen humans and bring them back into relationship with Himself.

It has been said that the "Old Testament is the New Testament Concealed; the New Testament is the Old Testament revealed." The Bible describes history *before it happens*. It comes to us from outside the dimensions of space and time. Of course, in making these statements, an astute observer will correctly point out that we are using the Bible to support itself. However, in this case it works, because what we have in our hands is demonstrably the perfect Word of God as presented to humanity. If you have any doubts about this, consider the following observations about Scripture. Note that this is a short list and not complete, but it will do for our purposes.

Archaeological Evidence

Every archaeological discovery ever made has supported the Old Testament and New Testament documents. When a new finding from an archaeological study comes out, many nonbelievers overreact because they think the discovery reveals something that contradicts Scripture. Ultimately, these individuals are always proved wrong.

For example, consider the story about the pool of Bethesda near the Sheep Gate in Jerusalem as recounted in the gospel of John. In the account, John describes a pool where many sick people would gather and lie around day and night to wait for an angel to stir the waters. When the people saw a disturbance, they would rush into the pool. The first one in was healed. Many non-believing archaeologists made light of this story. They said it could not be true, because such a place never existed. Then in 1964, archaeologists discovered the remains of Byzantine and Crusader churches built over the top of the healing pools. The discoveries silenced the critics.

Historical Authenticity

The documents of the New Testament and the Old Testament are the most reliable writings we have available to us today in terms of their historicity. In fact, we can be more certain of their authenticity than we can be of the evening news. For example, the following passage in Isaiah was written more than seven hundred years before the birth of Jesus Christ:

> My servant grew up in the Lord's presence like a tender green shoot, sprouting from a root in dry and sterile ground. There was nothing beautiful or majestic about his appearance, nothing to attract us to him. He was despised and rejected—a man of sorrows, acquainted with bitterest grief. We turned our backs on him and looked the other way when he went by. He was despised, and we did not care. . . . He was wounded and crushed for our sins. He was beaten that we might have peace. He was whipped, and we were healed! . . . He was oppressed and treated harshly, yet he never said a word. He was led as a lamb to the slaughter. And as a sheep is silent before the shearers, he did not open his mouth. From prison and trial they led him away to his death. But who among the people realized that he was dying for their sins—that he was suffering their punishment? He had done no wrong, and he never deceived anyone. But he was buried like a criminal; he was put in a rich man's grave.
>
> —Isaiah 53:2-3, 5, 7-9 NLT

Do you see how God reveals to us the authenticity of His Word? This prophecy speaks of the coming Messiah in terms that could only be fulfilled by Jesus Christ. What is interesting is that you will find this passage in the *middle of the Old Testament.* Skeptical Jewish rabbis and scholars used to claim that this prophecy had been inserted into the text many years after the birth of Jesus. However, when archaeologists discovered some of the oldest copies of Isaiah in existence in a find known as the Dead Sea Scrolls, there was chapter 53 right where it was supposed to be: in the middle of the text. These skeptical teachers were chagrined and had to admit that the findings proved the passage was prophesying about the coming of Christ, the Messiah to the Jewish peoples.

Mathematic Certainty

Finally, we can be sure that the Bible is true because findings show that it is mathematically impossible for it to be untrue. No other religion can claim this of their sacred writings. In fact, it is inaccurate to call Christianity a "religion," because in actuality it is a personal relationship with God made possible through the person of Jesus Christ. We will look at some of these undeniable mathematical proofs of the authenticity of the Judeo-Christian Scriptures in greater depth in the next section, beginning with a brief examination of composite probability theory.

COMPOSITE PROBABILITY THEORY

If something has a 1 in 10 chance of occurring, that is easy for us to understand. It means that 10 percent of the time, the event will happen. However, when we combine the probability of different events occurring at the same time, the odds of that event actually taking place goes down exponentially. This is the basic premise behind composite probability theory.

If two events have a 1 in 10 chance of happening, the chance that both of these will occur is 1 in 10 x 10, or 1 in 100. To show this numerically, this probability would be 1 in 10^2, with the 1 in superscript indicating how many tens are being multiplied. If we have 10^3, it means that we have a number of 1,000. Thus, 10^4 is equivalent to 10,000, and so on. This is referred to as 10 to the first power, 10 to the second power, 10 to the third power, and so on.

We can apply this model to the prophecy revealed in the Bible to figure out the mathematical chances of Jesus' birth, life, and death, in addition to many other events occurring in the New Testament by chance. To demonstrate this, we will consider eight prophecies about Jesus and assign a probability of them occurring individually by chance. To eliminate any disagreement, we will be more limiting than necessary. Furthermore, we will use the prophecies that are arguably the most unlikely to be fulfilled by chance. I think you will agree that in doing so, we are severely handicapping ourselves.

Here is the first prophecy from Micah 5:2: "But you, O Bethlehem Ephrathah, are only a small village in Judah. Yet a ruler of Israel will come from you, one whose origins are from the distant past" (NLT). This prophecy tells us that the Messiah will be born in Bethlehem. What is the chance of that actually occurring? As we consider this, we also have to ask: What is the probability that anyone in the history of the world might be born in this obscure town? When we take into account all the people who ever lived, this might conservatively be 1 in 200,000.

Let's move on to the second prophecy in Zechariah 9:9: "Rejoice greatly, O people of Zion! Shout in triumph, O people of Jerusalem! Look, your king is coming to you. He is righteous and victorious, yet he is humble, riding on a donkey—even on a donkey's colt" (NLT). For our purposes, we can assume that the chance that the Messiah (the king) riding into Jerusalem on a donkey might be 1 in 100. But, really, how many kings in the history of the world have actually done this?

The third prophecy is from Zechariah 11:12: "I said to them, 'If you like, give me my wages, whatever I am worth; but only if you want to.' So they counted out for my wages thirty pieces of silver" (NLT). What is the chance that someone would be betrayed and that the price of that betrayal would be thirty pieces of silver? For our purposes, let's assume the chance that anyone in the history of the world would be betrayed for thirty pieces of silver might be 1 in 1,000.

The fourth prophecy comes from Zechariah 11:13: "The Lord said to me, 'Throw it to the potters'—this magnificent sum at which they valued me! So I took the thirty coins and threw them to the potters in the Temple of the Lord." Now we need to consider what the chances would be that a Temple and a potter would be involved in someone's betrayal. For our statistical model, let's assume this is 1 in 100,000.

The fifth prophecy in Zechariah 13:6 reads: "And one shall say unto him, What are these wounds in thine hands? Then he shall answer, Those with which I was wounded in the house of my friends" (KJV). The question here is, "How many people in the history of the world have died with wounds in their hands?" I believe we can safely assume that the chance of any person dying with wounds in his or her hands is somewhat greater than 1 in 1,000.

The sixth prophecy in Isaiah 53:7 states, "He was oppressed and treated harshly, yet he never said a word. He was led as a lamb to the slaughter. And as a sheep is silent before the shearers, he did not open his mouth" (NLT). This raises a particularly tough question. How many people in the history of the world can we imagine being put on trial, knowing that they were innocent, without making one statement in their defense? For our statistical model, let's say this is 1 in 1,000, although it is pretty hard to imagine.

Moving on to the seventh prophecy, in Isaiah 53:9 we read, "He had done no wrong and had never deceived anyone. But he was buried like a criminal; he was put in a rich man's grave" (NLT). Here we need to consider how many people, out of all the good individuals in the world who have died, have died a criminal's death and been buried in a rich person's grave? These people died out of place. (Some might also infer that they were buried out of place, though that is not necessarily true.) Let's assume that the chance of a good person dying as a criminal and being buried with the rich is about 1 in 1,000.

The eighth and final prophecy is from Psalm 22:16: "My enemies surround me like a pack of dogs; an evil gang closes in on me. They have pierced my hands and feet" (NLT). Remember that this passage and all the other prophetic references to the crucifixion were written before this form of execution was even invented. However, for our purposes, we just need to consider the probability of someone in the history of the world being crucified in this way. Certainly, Jesus wasn't the only person killed by crucifixion. We will say that the chances of a person dying from this specific form of execution to be at 1 in 10,000.

Calculating the Results

To determine the chance that all these things would happen to the same person by chance, we simply multiply the fraction of each of the eight probabilities. When we do, we get a chance of 1 in 10^{28}. In other words, the probability is 1 in 10,000,000,000,000,000,000,000,000,000. Would you bet against these odds?

Unfortunately, there is another blow coming for those who do not believe that the Bible is true or that Jesus is who He said He was. There are not just eight prophecies of this nature in the Bible that were fulfilled in Jesus Christ—there are *more than three hundred* such prophecies in the Old Testament. The prophecies we looked at were just the ones that we could most easily show fulfilled.

If we deal with only forty-eight prophecies about Jesus, based on the above numbers, the chance that Jesus is not who He said He was or that the Bible is not true is 1 in 10^{168}. This is a larger number than most of us can grasp (though you may want to try to write it sometime). To give you some perspective on just how big this number is, consider these statistics:

1. If the state of Texas were buried in silver dollars two feet deep, it would be covered by 10^{17} silver dollars.
2. In the history of the world, only 10^{11} people have supposedly ever lived. (I don't know who counted this.)
3. There are 10^{17} seconds in one billion years.
4. Scientists tell us that there are 10^{66} atoms in the universe and 10^{80} particles in the universe.
5. Looking at just forty-eight prophecies out of more than three hundred, there is only a 1 in 10^{168} chance of Jesus not being who He said He was or the Bible being wrong.

In probability theory, the threshold for an occurrence being absurd—translate that as "impossible"—is only 10^{50}. No thinking person who understands these simple probabilities can deny the reality of our faith or the Bible based on intellect. Every person who has set out to disprove the Judeo-Christian Scriptures on an empirical basis has ended up proving the Bible's authenticity and has, in most cases, become a believer.

These facts are more certain than any others in the world. However, not everyone who has come to realize the reliability and reality of these documents has become a believer. These intelligent people who understand the statistical impossibility that Jesus was not who He claimed to be and who yet do not make a decision for Christ are not insane; they generally just have embedded emotional issues. They allow these issues to stop them from enjoying the many experiential benefits that God offers through His Word and the dynamic relationship they could have with Him, not to mention longer-term benefits. These people, of course, deserve love and prayer, because this is not just a matter of the intellect. If it were, every intelligent inquirer would be a believer. Rather, it is very much a matter of the heart, the emotions, and the spirit.

FOR STUDY AND REFLECTION

Consider the following questions based on the material you read in this chapter:

1. What are some of the theories for how the Koran was written? What is the significance of the alphanumeric message hidden in the text of the Koran?

2. What are some of the factual errors found in the Koran? What are some of the most likely reasons for how these errors made it into the Koran?

3. What are some of the sources that Muhammad most likely drew from when creating his stories in the Koran?

4. What is the difference between the way the Bible was written and the Koran was written? What do the biblical writers say about adding to or modifying the text of the Bible?

5. What archaeological evidence do we have that the Bible is factual? What historical authenticity do we possess?

6. What is the composite probability theory? How does it relate to biblical prophecy in the Bible?

To conclude this chapter, I suggest you view the next ten minutes of *Jihad in America*. Play the video from just after the interview with Paul Bremer to the shot of the terrorist documents on the table (just before the interview with Michael

Cherkasky of the Manhattan District Attorney's office). After watching the video, consider the following questions:

1. Where did Abdullah Azzam (the speaker in Brooklyn, New York) say that *jihad* should be waged?

2. What did he say *jihad* meant?

3. What did Fayiz Azzam (the speaker in Atlanta) say that Allah's religion must offer?

4. Why do you feel that El Sayed Nosair, the Egyptian immigrant who was placed on trial for killing Meir Kahane, was acquitted of murder?

5. How is the problem with Islamic terrorism different from terrorism in the past?

CHAPTER SIX

ALLAH AND THE GOD OF THE JEWISH AND CHRISTIAN SCRIPTURES

THE AVERAGE MUSLIM today believes that Allah and the Judeo-Christian God are one and the same. However, a scholarly examination of the venerated writings of Islam, Judaism, and Christianity is necessary to come to a correct conclusion in this matter.

One would assume that if the God of the Judeo-Christian Scriptures and Allah were the same, their representatives would speak and act consistently. But is that the case? Do the words and deeds of Muhammad, who claimed to be the latest and greatest of all the prophets, match up with the words and deeds of Christ, who said He was the Son of God? We have excellent examples from the Hadith and the Bible that allow us to determine how the two men responded to one particular issue: adultery.

Muhammad's teachings and views on adultery can be found in the following Hadith as reported by Imran b. Husain, one of the companions of Muhammad:

A woman came to Muhammad and said, "I have committed adultery, so purify me." Muhammad told her, "Go away until you give birth to the child." After she gave birth, she returned with the child and said, "Here is the child I have given birth to." Muhammad answered, "Go away and nurse him until you wean him." When she had weaned him, she came to Muhammad with the child, who was holding a piece of bread in his hand. The woman said, "Allah's Apostle, here is he, as I have weaned him and eats food." Muhammad gave the child to one of the Muslims and then pronounced punishment. The woman was buried in a ditch up to her chest and the people stoned her.[1]

From this account we see that Muhammad was clearly opposed to adultery, and throughout the Koran we repeatedly find warnings against committing the act: "Do not go anywhere near adultery: it is an outrage, and an evil path" (Sura 17:32). What is interesting is that Muhammad showed no mercy for the woman who had come to him and confessed her transgression. This tells us a great deal about Muhammad's views on sin, forgiveness, and repentance. It also enlightens us about the prophet's love and concern for those whom he called his people. By extension, this also tells us about Allah, as Muhammad claimed to be his true representative on the earth.

THE MERCY OF CHRIST

Now, let's compare this account to a similar story we find in the Judeo-Christian Scriptures. Clearly, Jesus was also opposed to adultery. In fact, He took it a step further, saying, "You have heard that it was said to those of old, 'You shall not commit adultery.' But I say to you that whoever looks at a woman to lust for her has already committed adultery with her in his heart" (Matt. 5:27-28 NKJV). The difference, however, is in how Jesus treated the person who had been caught committing the act, as the following story relates:

As he was speaking, the teachers of religious law and Pharisees brought a woman they had caught in the act of adultery. They put her in front of the crowd. "Teacher," they said to Jesus, "this woman was caught in the very act of adultery. The law of Moses says to stone her. What do you say?" They were trying to trap him into saying something they could use against him, but Jesus stooped down and wrote in the dust with his finger. They kept demanding an answer, so he stood up again and said, "All right, stone her. But let those who have never sinned throw the first stones!" Then he stooped down again and wrote in the dust. When the accusers heard this, they slipped away one by one, beginning with the oldest, until only Jesus was left in the middle of the crowd with the woman. Then Jesus stood up again and said to her, "Where are your accusers? Didn't even one of them condemn you?" "No, Lord," she said. And Jesus said, "Neither do I. Go and sin no more."

—John 8:3-11 NLT

Unlike Muhammad, Jesus showed mercy toward the woman. When the teachers of the law and the Pharisees condemned her, Jesus calmly pointed out that all have sinned under the law and deserve God's punishment (see Rom. 3:23). However, as John 3:17 states, "God did not send his Son into the world to condemn the world, but to save the world through him" (NIV). Jesus' mission was to save those who were lost in sin and bring them back into relationship with God. In doing so, He showed mercy to those who were repentant of their sins and forgave them for their transgressions. This reveals a great deal to us about the character of the God of the Judeo-Christian Scriptures. It shows us how He views sin, forgiveness, and repentance, and how He cares about those whom He calls His people.

We see further evidence of these traits throughout the gospel accounts. In Matthew 15:32, Jesus showed compassion for the crowd because they were hungry. In Matthew 20:34, He showed compassion for two blind men—outcasts of society—who were sitting by the roadside. He was moved to pity in Mark 1:40 when two lepers approached Him and asked to be healed, and in Mark 6:34 He was concerned about those who were hungry for the Word of God and "like sheep without a shepherd." In these and many other ways, Jesus revealed God's incredible love for people. As the psalmist wrote in Psalm 136:2, "Oh, give thanks to the God of gods! For His mercy endures forever."

In Sura 2:23, Muhammad characterized himself and other Muslims as slaves of Allah. Allah was at the head, Muhammad the prophet was the focus, and all others were either fellow slaves or evil unbelievers. In this sense, Allah is unknowable, impersonal, unreliable, and untrustworthy—a deity who only judges and punishes for sin: "If they reject your judgment, know that it is Allah's wish that you scourge them for their sins" (Sura 5:49). Jesus, with the Father at the head and Himself in the middle, characterized believers as God's children and unbelievers as lost sheep. The difference can be depicted as follows:

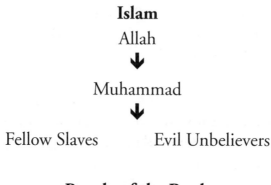

Islam
Allah
↓
Muhammad
↓
Fellow Slaves   Evil Unbelievers

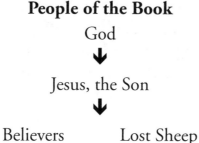

People of the Book
God
↓
Jesus, the Son
↓
Believers   Lost Sheep

WHO IS ALLAH?

Today, you often see Muslims on television shouting, "Allah Akbar!" The correspondents on CNN tell us that this phrase means, "God is great." Actually, *Allah Akbar* means, "Allah is greater"—specifically that he is greater than the God of Abraham, Isaac, and Jacob. (Interestingly, Isaiah 14:12-15 tells us that Satan made the same claim.) Muslims who understand their religion know that Allah differs from the Judeo-Christian God, though they do not understand who he truly represents.

So if the God of the Jews and Christians is not the same as that of the Muslims, then who exactly *is* Allah? To find the answer to this question, we must return to the time of Muhammad and examine the culture in which he lived. As we discussed, Mecca was the center of all pagan religions in Arabia and the home of 360 idols. These idols were housed in a cube-like temple called the Ka'aba.

Muslims claim that the Ka'aba was built by Abraham and Ishmael, though as you might expect, there is no evidence to support this assertion. (History shows that Ishmael was sent away before he was old enough to engage in helping construct a building.) Muslims claim that the stone was originally white, but that one day when Abraham and Ishmael were sitting on it, the stone suddenly turned black because of the people's sins. (Remember, practitioners of Islam describe sin in a way that is opposite to the way in which the Judeo-Christian Scriptures define it.)

History reveals that the Ka'aba was actually built by the Sabeans, the predecessors to the Muslims, who lived in what is today the country of Yemen. The Sabeans built the Ka'aba around a big black stone that scholars believe was a meteorite. To the pagan worshipers, the Ka'aba marked the location where the divine world intersected the earth. It was believed to be the center of the world, with the Gate of Heaven directly above it. The black meteorite stone was a symbol of this link: it had fallen from the sky to the earth, thereby linking the two worlds.[2] The pagans bowed and prayed toward Mecca because *the big black stone and their idols were there*. Each tribe had its own idol or idols, and each had a similar tradition.

Once each year, tribes from all around the Arabian Peninsula made pilgrimages to Mecca to pay homage to the various gods in the temple. When they arrived, the pilgrims ran around the big black stone seven times and then kissed it. After kissing the stone, they ran to a place called the Wadi Mina to throw stones at the devil. No one is sure how this tradition began, but some believe the pilgrims performed these rites to ensure the temporary forgiveness of their sins. Muslims perform these same acts today during the *hajj*. However, for them, this act has nothing to do with whether they go to their form of paradise, as the only way they can be assured of reaching their version of heaven is by dying in a *jihad*.

Around AD 500, the Ka'aba came under the protection and care of the Quraysh tribe, which, as you may recall, was the tribe into which Muhammad was later born. As caretakers of the temple, the Quraysh tribe collected the pilgrims' offerings of money, food, animals and whatever else they wanted to give to the idols and kept those offerings for themselves. For them, it was quite a profitable business model. Over time, the Quraysh tribe grew rich and established a caravan business with a base in Mecca.

AL-ILAH, THE MOON GOD

The primary god and ruler of the 360 other gods—the "Lord of the Ka'aba"—was Al-ilah, the moon god. Over time, the name "Al-ilah" was contracted into "Allah." Although some credit Muhammad with changing the name, the fact that "Allah" was in his father's and uncle's names shows that this change had already occurred by the time Muhammad was born. During the month of Ramadan, worshipers of Al-ilah would fast during the daylight hours from crescent moon to crescent moon—a similar ritual that Muslims perform today during the month of Ramadan.

Different cultures of the time referred to Al-ilah by different names. In Sumer, a region in southern Mesopotamia just north of Arabia, the moon god was called Hubal. About four hundred years before the birth of Muhammad, a man with a very long name (Amr ibn Lahya ibn Harath ibn 'Amru l-Qays ibn Thalaba ibn Azd ibn Khalan ibn Babalyun ibn Saba) put an idol of Hubal on the roof of the Ka'aba. This was one of the chief deities of the Quraysh tribe, and they referred to the temple as the "House of the Moon God." Later, during the time of Muhammad, Allah replaced this god, and the Ka'aba became known as the "House of Allah."

In the Mesopotamian religion, the moon god, or "controller of the night," was called Sin. This god was described as a "fierce young bull, thick of horns, perfect of limbs, with a beautiful bird of blue." The symbol for this god was a crescent moon, with the tips of the two horns representing the two tips of the moon.

Nabonidus, the last king of the Neo-Babylonian Empire, who reigned from 556–539 BC, promoted Sin to the top of the Babylonian pantheon to make the Babylonian religion more acceptable to the Arabians and Aramaeans. The Arabians held the moon god in esteem, but they had more difficulty identifying with Marduk, the supreme Babylonian deity largely associated with the city of Babylon. The Muslims adopted this crescent moon as the symbol for Islam—it appears on the flag of Saudi Arabia along with a sword.

The worship of the moon god was occurring in many different cultures before the birth of Muhammad. With Mecca situated at the crossroads of these different cultures, it was easy for Muhammad to learn about the different customs, package them together, and make them part of his political system to achieve power. At the heart of it, this is what happened: Muhammad successfully packaged himself as a priest-king. He built a religious system that incorporated the beliefs of many different groups and used that system as a method of conquest.

The fact that idol worship was widespread at the time actually helps to explain why Muhammad's "new" religion was so rapidly and readily accepted by the populace. All Muhammad had to do was transform a polytheistic form of heathenism into a monotheistic form of heathenism, incorporating pagan beliefs about *jinns,* fairies, spells, magic stones, fetishes, and animalistic beliefs into Islam to ensure its success (see Sura 55, 72, 113, and 114). This ultimately allowed the people to believe whatever they believed before, as long as they submitted to the authority of Allah and Muhammad (and paid Muhammad his annual tribute).

A Warning Against Idols

Surprising to many, these ancient pagan religious practices that Muhammad packaged into Islam are also spoken of in the Old Testament. Here are a few of the places in the Bible where God warns His people not to worship any of these pagan gods:

When you look up into the sky and see the sun, moon, and stars—all the forces of heaven—don't be seduced by them and worship them. The LORD your God designated these heavenly bodies for all the peoples of the earth.

—Deut. 4:19 NLT

Suppose a man or woman among you, in one of your towns that the LORD your God is giving you, has done evil in the sight of the LORD your God and has violated the covenant by serving other gods or by worshiping the sun, the moon, or any of the forces of heaven, which I have strictly forbidden. When you hear about it, investigate the matter thoroughly. If it is true that this detestable thing has been done in Israel, then that man or woman must be taken to the gates of the town and stoned to death.

—Deut. 17:2-5 NLT

He did away with the pagan priests, who had been appointed by the previous kings of Judah, for they had burned incense at the pagan shrines throughout Judah and even in the vicinity of Jerusalem. They had also offered incense to Baal, and to the sun, the moon, the constellations, and to all the forces of heaven.

—2 Kings 23:5 NLT

Have I looked at the sun shining in the skies, or the moon walking down its silver pathway, and been secretly enticed in my heart to worship them? If so, I should be punished by the judges, for it would mean I had denied the God of heaven.

—Job 31:26-28 NLT

How unbelievably brainless we human beings can be to be enticed to worship these inanimate and created objects.

NOT JUST ANY GOLDEN CALF

In Genesis 11:27-31, we read that Abraham and his nephew Lot were originally from the land of Ur, an ancient Sumerian city in the land of Mesopotamia. The spiritual ruler of Ur was the moon god, the same personage as the god of the Ka'aba. This is the background out of which God called Abraham to be the father of a new nation, which should give us some insight as to why the Israelites had trouble with idols and worshiping pagan deities.

Exodus 32 relates a story that illustrates this point. The Hebrews had recently been freed from bondage in the land of Egypt and were camped at Mount Sinai. Moses had gone up the mountain with Joshua, and he had been gone for a long time—so long, in fact, that the people thought he wasn't coming back. So they approached Aaron, Moses' brother, and asked him to make a god who would go before them and lead them out of the wilderness. Aaron agreed to go along with their plan.

So Aaron said, "Tell your wives and sons and daughters to take off their gold earrings, and then bring them to me." All the people obeyed Aaron and brought him their gold earrings. Then Aaron took the gold, melted it down, and molded and tooled it into the shape of a calf. The people exclaimed, "O Israel, these are the gods who brought you out of Egypt!" When Aaron saw how excited the people were about it, he built an altar in front of the calf and announced, "Tomorrow there will be a festival to the LORD!" So the people got up early the next morning to sacrifice burnt offerings and peace offerings. After this, they celebrated with feasting and drinking, and indulged themselves in pagan revelry.

—Exodus 32:2-6 NLT

Back up on the mountain, God saw what was going on and told Moses to get back down to the camp. He said that the people had defiled themselves by making an idol shaped like a calf and were saying, "These are your gods, O Israel, who brought you out of Egypt." As you will recall, the Mesopotamian moon god, Sin, was depicted as a bull, and the Egyptians and many of their neighbors in the ancient Middle East likewise worshiped the bull as a moon god. God was so angered by the people's actions that He wanted to destroy them. Only Moses' intercession on their behalf saved the Israelite race. Later in the story, Moses confronts the people about the gravity of their sin and what it would mean for them:

The next day Moses said to the people, "You have committed a terrible sin, but I will return to the LORD on the mountain. Perhaps I will be able to obtain forgiveness for you." So Moses returned to the LORD and said, "Alas, these people have committed a terrible sin. They have made gods of gold for themselves. But now, please forgive their sin—and if not, then blot me out of the record you are keeping." The LORD replied to Moses, "I will blot out whoever has sinned against me. Now go, lead the people to the place I told you about. Look! My angel will lead the way before you! But when I call the people to account, I will certainly punish them for their sins." And the LORD sent a great plague upon the people because they had worshiped the calf Aaron had made.

—Ex. 32:30-35

In Acts 7:39-43, when Stephen explained the story of the golden calf to the members of the Sanhedrin, he illuminated exactly what it was that God had given the people over to as a result of their idol worship:

But our ancestors rejected Moses and wanted to return to Egypt. They told Aaron, "Make us some gods who can lead us, for we don't know what has become of this Moses, who brought us out of Egypt." So they made an idol shaped like a *calf*, and they sacrificed to it and rejoiced in this thing they had made. Then God turned away from them and gave them up to serve the sun, *moon*, and stars as their gods! In the book of the prophets it is written, "Was it to me you were bringing sacrifices during those forty years in the wilderness, Israel? No, your real interest was in your pagan gods—the shrine of Molech, the star god Rephan, and the images you made to worship them. So I will send you into captivity far away in Babylon."

—NLT, emphasis added

The Israelites struggled with the worship of the moon god throughout their history. After the people had taken the land of Canaan and established a monarchy, King Solomon, the successor to King David, built a palace and filled it with extravagant items of gold and silver. He also made an ivory throne and overlaid it with the finest gold. "The throne had six steps, and at the back of the throne was a *calf's head*, and on each side of the seat were armrests and two lions standing beside the armrests" (1 Kings 10:19 ESV, emphasis added). Later, after the kingdom was divided, King Jeroboam led the nation of Israel away from the worship of the one true God:

So on the advice of his counselors, the king made *two gold calves*. He said to the people, "It is too much trouble for you to worship in Jerusalem. O Israel, these are the gods who brought you out of Egypt!" He placed these *calf idols* at the southern and northern ends of Israel—in Bethel and in Dan. This became a great sin, for the people worshiped them, traveling even as far as Dan.

—1 Kings 12:38-30 NLT, emphasis added

In making this declaration, Jeroboam was echoing the words of Aaron that it was the gods represented by the calf idols that had led the people out of Egypt. He appointed "his own priests to serve at the pagan shrines, where they worshiped the goat and *calf idols* he had made" (2 Chron. 11:15 NLT). Jeroboam's successors tended to follow his error. Time and again the people of Israel turned their back on the Lord and worshiped the gods of the sun, moon, and stars. Eventually, God sent prophets to warn the people of their fate if they did not abandon these false gods:

> The people have appointed kings and princes, but not with my consent. By making idols for themselves from their silver and gold, they have brought about their own destruction. O Samaria, I reject this *calf*—this idol you have made. My fury burns against you. How long will you be incapable of innocence? This *calf* you worship was crafted by your own hands! It is not God! Therefore, it must be smashed to bits.
>
> —Hos. 8:4-6 NLT, emphasis added

> The people of Samaria tremble for their *calf idol* at Beth-aven. The people mourn over it, and the priests wail for it, because its glory will be stripped away. This idol they love so much will be carted away with them when they go as captives to Assyria, a gift to the great king there. Israel will be laughed at and shamed because its people have trusted in this idol.
>
> —Hos. 10:5-6 NLT, emphasis added

> The people of Ephraim sinned by worshiping Baal and thus sealed their destruction. Now they keep on sinning by making silver idols to worship—images shaped skillfully with human hands. "Sacrifice to these," they cry, "and kiss the *calf idols*!" Therefore, they will disappear like the morning mist, like dew in the morning sun, like chaff blown by the wind, like smoke from a chimney.
>
> —Hos. 13:1-3 NLT, emphasis added

> The Lord gave these messages to Zephaniah when Josiah son of Amon was king of Judah. . . . "I will put an end to all the idolatrous priests, so that even the memory of them will disappear. For they go up to their roofs and bow to the sun, *moon,* and stars. They claim to follow the Lord, but then they worship Molech, too. So now I will destroy them!"
>
> —Zeph. 1:1, 4-5 NLT, emphasis added

We also find in the Tanakh that God doesn't like certain types of jewelry. While at first glance it might seem strange that God is singling these items out, when we understand the problem the Israelites had with worshiping the moon god, it brings these passages into greater focus. In Judges 8:21, Gideon "arose and killed Zebah and Zalmunna, and took the *crescent ornaments* which were on their camels' necks" (NASB, emphasis added).

Zebah and Zalmunna were the kings of the Midianites, who had invaded the land of Canaan and were oppressing the Israelites. After killing these kings, Gideon collected the jewelry from the Midianites, and "the weight of the gold earrings was forty-three pounds, not including the *crescents* and pendants, the royal clothing of the kings, or the chains around the necks of their camels" (Judges 8:26 NLT, emphasis added). The prophet Isaiah also spoke of this type of jewelry: "The Lord will strip away their artful beauty—their ornaments, headbands, and *crescent* necklaces" (Isaiah 3:18 NLT, emphasis added).

The ancient camel drivers put symbols on their camels (crescents) much like some in our society put symbols (bumper stickers) on our cars. The crescent symbol represented worship of the moon god. No wonder the God of Abraham, Isaac, and Jacob found displaying such symbols shameful. Pray that those deceived by the misconceptions about Allah will have their eyes, minds, and hearts opened to the truth.

FOR STUDY AND REFLECTION

From the evidence presented in this chapter, it is apparent that Allah and the God of the Judeo-Christian Scriptures are not the same. We see this in the actions of their representatives on earth: Muhammad, Allah's "greatest prophet" in Islam, and Jesus, the Son of God in Christianity.

Consider the following questions based on the material you read in this chapter:

1. What does the way in which Muhammad treated the woman caught in adultery teach us about Allah's view of sin, forgiveness, and repentance?

2. What does the way in which Jesus treated the woman caught in adultery teach us about God's view of sin, forgiveness, and repentance?

3. What evidence do we find that leads to the conclusion that Allah is not the same as the God of the Judeo-Christian Scriptures?

4. Who was Al-ilah? In what ways is this entity depicted in other Mesopotamian religions? What references to this being do we find in the Bible?

5. How did Muhammad use Al-ilah and other traditions of the time to build support for his religion of Islam?

6. Child sacrifice was part of ancient pagan religions. Is it reasonable to draw a comparison with the Muslims today who are willing to send their children on suicide bombing missions of death? Why or why not?

7. Someone noted that if Satan designed a religion, Islam would be it. How do you feel about this statement?

To conclude this chapter, I suggest you view the next ten minutes of *Jihad in America*. Play the video from the interview with Michael Cherkasky to just after the speech by Sheik Abdul Wali Zindani. After watching the clip, consider the following questions:

1. With what types of activities have the groups shown in the video been involved in America?

2. What does Zindani call the enemies of Allah?

3. Why is this statement ironic, given what you have learned from this chapter?

4. Does this excerpt from the video bring other questions to mind?

Note that Ramzi Yousef, the man in this excerpt who built the device used in the World Trade Center bombing, was finally located. After leaving the United States, he was involved in the bombing of a Japanese airliner. From there he went to the Philippines, where he made bombs in an upper-story apartment. One day, when he was cooking up a "batch" on the stove, it caught fire, and he panicked. Yousef dove out the window to the fire escape and ran away. Much to his surprise, the apartment did not blow up, but a large fire did get under way. The fire department was called in, and when they extinguished the blaze, they found Yousef's still-intact computer. The authorities examined Yousef's hard drive, where they found the references and contact information they needed to find Yousef and his compatriots and put them in jail.

CHAPTER SEVEN

THE JESUS OF ISLAM AND THE JESUS OF THE BIBLE

NOW THAT WE have examined the differences between Allah and the God of the Jewish and Christian Scriptures, we need to take a look at how Islam treats Jesus, the Messiah whom Christians believe to be the Son of God. Jesus is mentioned twenty-five times in the Koran, where He is depicted as a messenger of God who was sent to guide the Jews with a new Scripture (the gospel). Jesus is considered to have been one who submitted to the will of God and taught that everyone should follow the "straight path" as commanded by God. Muslims also believe that Jesus was born to Mary, a virgin, and that He performed miracles. All of this seems to fit the depiction of Jesus that we find in gospel accounts of Matthew, Mark, Luke, and John. However, this is where the similarities end.

In the Koran, Jesus is viewed as just another prophet. While it is true that He could perform miracles, Muslims believe this ability was given by permission of God rather than through His own authority as the Son of God. They do not accept the validity of passages such as Mark 2:5-12, where Jesus tells a paralyzed man that He has the authority to forgive the man's sins because He is God. In fact, most of the times when Jesus is mentioned, the verse is preceded by the words, "Jesus, the son of Mary." This is to emphasize that Muslims do not believe Jesus is the Son of God.[1]

Also, according to the Koran, Jesus was not killed or crucified, and He never atoned for the sins of mankind. "The Messiah, son of Mary, was only a messenger; messengers before him had indeed passed away" (Sura 5:75). The Koran states that the Jews and the Romans sought to kill Christ but did not, though "it appeared so unto them" (Sura 4:157). The reason why it appeared that they had killed Jesus is because Allah raised Him up into heaven. In other words, instead of dying and being resurrected and *then* ascending into heaven (as we read in Acts 1:9), Allah took Jesus directly up to paradise in bodily form.

Muslims claim that Muhammad, during one of his epileptic fits, flew up to heaven (perhaps on his famous winged donkey) and asked Jesus if he was truly the Son of God. Muhammad said that Jesus replied no, He was not, and that Muhammad was the greatest prophet. Muslims believe that Jesus will say the same thing on the Day of Judgment. At that point, Allah will vindicate Him (see Sura 3:55).

JESUS IN THE KORAN

There are a number of other invented stories about Jesus that appear in the Koran. Because the Koran is not arranged in chronological order, these stories appear throughout the book in various places. For instance, if you read the Koran in the normal order, you will find Jesus mentioned along with Moses in Sura 2, and then read the story of His birth in Sura 19. This is perhaps because by some accounts the Koran is essentially a two-part book, with the earlier chapters allegedly written from Muhammad's base in Mecca from AD 610–622 and the later chapters allegedly written from Medina from AD 622–634.[2]

In the account depicting Christ's birth in Sura 19, Mary goes out alone into the desert to give birth to Jesus, where she finds a dead palm tree. As she is resting against the tree, the angel Gabriel appears and creates a small river under her from which she can drink. Gabriel also instructs her to shake the palm tree and it will turn green and provide her with dates. Later that day, Mary gives birth to Jesus. Forty days later, she takes Him back to her people.

Muslims claim that as an infant, Jesus spoke from the crib and told the people that Allah would reveal "the Book" (the gospel) to Him and make Him a prophet (see Sura 19:29-33). He is said to have made clay birds live and breathe (see Sura 5:21). Later, after Jesus began His ministry, He was aided by a group of disciples (who go unnamed in the Koran). In one story, these disciples begin to question their belief, so they ask for a laden table to be sent from heaven to offer proof that Jesus is preaching the true message of God:

> Behold! The disciples, said: "O Jesus the son of Mary! Can thy Lord send down to us a table set (with viands) from heaven?" Said Jesus: "Fear Allah, if ye have faith." They said: "We only wish to eat thereof and satisfy our hearts, and to know that thou hast indeed told us the truth; and that we ourselves may be witnesses to the miracle." Said Jesus the son of Mary: "O Allah our Lord! Send us from heaven a table set (with viands), that there may be for us—for the first and the last of us—a solemn festival and a sign from thee; and provide for our sustenance, for thou art the best Sustainer (of our needs)." Allah said: "I will send it down unto you: But if any of you after that resisteth faith, I will punish him with a penalty such as I have not inflicted on any one among all the peoples."
>
> —Sura 5:112-115

There is also a story in Islam about what Jesus will do on the Day of Judgment. According to the Hadith, when Jesus comes back to earth, He will return as a Muslim. (Actually, followers of Islam believe that Jesus was a true Muslim all along.) He will set down to earth on the Golan Heights and face off against the Antichrist, who is a Jew, in battle. Jesus will kill the Antichrist with a spear and then go up to the temple mount to pray with 400,000 other Muslims.

Once on the temple mount, Jesus and the Muslims will break all the crosses and destroy all the synagogues and churches. Jesus will slit the throats of all the Jews and Christians who will not convert to Islam. On that day, some of the Jews will temporarily escape death and will hide behind the rocks and the trees. However, Allah will give voice to the rocks, and they will shout out, "There is a Jew hiding behind me, come and kill him!" On the Day of Judgment, every Jew on earth will be destroyed.

This depiction of Christ is vastly different from what we find in the Bible. Allah—the god who is depicted here—wants all the Jews dead. This is not the God of Abraham, Isaac and Jacob. Furthermore, the Bible is clear that God's enemy is Satan, and when Christ returns, He will destroy the kingdom of Satan on this earth. It will not be a bloodbath *directed at those who will not convert to Islam.* In all of the stories of Christ that appear in the Koran, Jesus does not offer forgiveness of sins. As a prophet, the Jesus of Islam is nothing. As the Son of God, He is everything.

JESUS AND JIHAD

Jesus told His disciples, "My Father's house has many rooms; if that were not so, would I have told you that I am going there to prepare a place for you? And if I go and prepare a place for you, I will come back and take you to be with me that you also may be where I am. You know the way to the place where I am going" (John 14:2-4 NIV). The "way" that Jesus said led to eternal life was through Him:

Jesus answered him, "I am the way, the truth, and the life. No one can come to the Father except through me."

—John 14:6 NLT

Peter replied, "Each of you must turn from your sins and turn to God, and be baptized in the name of Jesus Christ for the forgiveness of your sins. Then you will receive the gift of the Holy Spirit."

—Acts 2:38 NLT

He is the one all the prophets testified about, saying that everyone who believes in him will have their sins forgiven through his name.

—Acts 10:43 NLT

Then Jesus said, "Come to me, all of you who are weary and burdened and I will give you rest. Take my yoke upon you and learn from me, for I am gentle and humble in heart, and you will find rest for your souls. For my yoke is easy and my burden is light."

—Matt. 11:28-30

Do you remember the "One Way" sign popularized by Larry Norman, the "Father of Christian Rock and Roll"? The index finger is pointing up. Believers say that according to the Scriptures, there is only one way to heaven. Muslims also say there is only one way they can be certain *they* are going to heaven, which is to die in *jihad*. (Perhaps the sign for this would have to be a mock finger slice across the throat.) We find this teaching in Sura 61:10-13:

> Oh you who believe! Shall I guide you to a trade that will save you from a painful torment? That you believe in Allah and His Messenger [Muhammad] and that you strive hard and fight in the Cause of Allah with your wealth and your lives: that will be better for you, if you but know! (If you do so.) He will forgive you your sins and admit you into Gardens under which rivers flow and pleasant dwellings in paradise; that is indeed the great success. And (He will give you) another (blessing) which you love, help from Allah (against your enemies) and a near victory.

This reference has been taken by Muslims to mean that a person who dies in *jihad*—no matter how that term is defined—goes straight to paradise (and all the virgins waiting for him there). Islam is a religion of works where salvation is not assured unless one dies in *jihad*. Otherwise, a person's works are totaled up on a tally sheet and then read back on the Day of Judgment, when unreliable Allah decides one's fate. Dying in *jihad,* however, spares a person from this judgment and allows that individual to go straight to paradise with those waiting virgins.

Jihad is at the heart of every act of terrorism. The night before the hijackers flew the planes into the World Trade Center, they were out looking for prostitutes. This was perfectly acceptable according to their beliefs, because they were going to die in *jihad* the next day and go to their virgins in paradise. Furthermore, Muslims claim that Jesus also stated that believers go immediately to paradise if they take part in a *jihad*. They base this reasoning on a faulty interpretation of Jesus' words in Matthew 10:34-35 and Luke 12:51-52, where Christ states that He did not come to bring peace to the earth but a sword.

What Jesus was actually talking about here was the "sword" of division that God's Word brings—the division of truth from error and light from darkness (see Heb. 4:12). Christ doesn't call us to go to war in the same sense as jihad, but He does want us to make a difference in our society and in our culture. As He told His listeners in Matthew 5:14,16, "You are the light of the world . . . let your light shine before men, that they may see your good deeds and praise your Father in heaven." In 1 Corinthians 16:13, Paul told believers, "Be on your guard; stand firm in the faith; be men of courage; be strong."

We are to put our faith into action in all areas of life and stand up for what we know is right according to God's Word. We cannot be at peace with the evil we see around us.

THE INCLUSIVE GOSPEL

When we read about Jesus in the gospels, what we find is a man who was concerned about people from all walks of life. He didn't hang out with just the religious crowd or the social elite and neglect the poor, the destitute, the sick, the orphaned, and the demon-possessed. Instead, He came to save *all* sinners, regardless of what station in life they found themselves or what they had done in their past. The gospel of Jesus Christ is for all people and all nations.

It appears that the same is not true of Islam. In Sura 3:106-107, we read, "On the day when some faces will be whitened and some faces will be blackened, say to those whose faces will be blackened, 'Did ye reject faith after accepting it? Taste then the penalty for rejecting faith.' But those whose faces will be whitened, they will be in God's mercy: therein to dwell." According to Islam, only those with white faces will be saved, while those with black faces will be damned, punished, and killed. In this sense, white is equated with "goodness," while black is equated with "evil." This is a great deception that is occurring among black Muslims today.

There is much prejudice in the Muslim world, and this racism goes way back in history. In North Africa, the Saharan region used to be Christian before the arrival of the Muslims. Africa produced Christian theologians such as Augustine of Hippo (Algeria), Clement and Athanasius (Egypt), and Tertullian (Tunis). In Acts 8, we read how Ethiopia had a Christian community that was independent of the churches in Europe. However, all of this changed in AD 1275 when the

Muslims invaded and began to stamp out Christianity and enslave the population. In a *Time* magazine article, Robert Hughes states the following:

> The African slave trade as such, the black traffic, was an Arab invention, developed by traders with the enthusiastic collaboration of black African ones, institutionalized with the most unrelenting brutality, centuries before the white man appeared on the African continent, and continuing long after the slave market in North America was finally crushed. . . .

> Nothing in the writings of [Muhammad] forbids slavery, which is why it became such an Arab-dominated business. And the slave traffic could not have existed without the wholehearted cooperation of African tribal states, built on the supply of captives generated by their relentless wars. The image promulgated by pop-history fictions like *Roots*—of white slavers bursting with cutlass and musket into the settled lives of peaceful African villages—is very far from the historical truth. A marketing system had been in place for centuries, and its supply was controlled by Africans.

> Nor did it simply vanish with Abolition. Slave markets, supplying the Arab Emirates, were still operating in Djibouti in the 1950s; and since 1960, the slave trade has flourished in Mauritania and the Sudan. There are still reports of chattel slavery in northern Nigeria, Rwanda, and Niger.[3]

We see evidence of the prejudice of Muslims against those of other races in the recent events of the tsunami that hit the Far East in 2004. As you might recall, that tsunami struck numerous Muslim populations in nations around the Indian Ocean, killing more than 230,000 people and wreaking havoc wherever it struck. One of the countries hardest hit was Indonesia, of which 87 percent of the population is Muslim.[4]

Given this, you would think that the Muslim countries of the Middle East would rally to their Muslim brothers in a show of solidarity. However, the list of countries committing aid within two weeks of the disaster proved this was not the case:

- Japan, a country where Shintoism and Buddhism are the major religions, pledged $500 million.
- The United States pledged $350 million in public money and raised almost that much more from private donations.
- Saudi Arabia, the birthplace of Islam and a nation responsible for at least 10 percent of the world's oil production, pledged ten million dollars. That's right, only ten million dollars—and this was coming off one of the country's best years in profits.
- Tiny Qatar, a smaller Muslim nation, also pledged ten million dollars.
- Kuwait, another Islamic country, declined to pledge.
- The United Arab Emirates, an Islamic nation, declined to make a pledge.
- Iran, obviously a Muslim nation, also declined to pledge.
- Israel, the target of daily terrorism strikes from Muslim countries, pledged thirty-five million dollars—despite the fact that its economy was stretched to the brink from their defense budget. This amount is more than all of the Muslim countries combined. Israel also sent members of the Israeli defense forces to the area with tons of aid including food, tents, water containers, nylon sheeting, and medical supplies.[5]

The Muslim countries of the Middle East gave almost nothing to help their Muslim brothers. When asked why this was, Toronto Muslim leader and TV host Tarek Fatah said, "Dark-skinned Indian, Sri Lankan, Indonesian; truck drivers, cooks, and housekeepers; all children of a lesser God in the eyes of these Islamists of the Gulf." On CNN, representatives also stated that the reason the Muslims in the Middle East didn't support the Muslims in the Far East was because they were not faithful enough to Islam to warrant their aid.

MESSAGES TO THE WORLD

The Bible tells us that "the Son of Man came to seek and to save the lost" (Luke 19:10 NIV). Jesus came to fulfill the promises God had given to Abraham and His descendants (see Genesis 17), but when He died and was raised from the dead, He opened the way for everyone—both Jews and Gentiles—to enter into that covenant. "There is neither Jew nor Greek, there is neither slave nor free, there is neither male nor female; for you are all one in Christ Jesus. And if you are Christ's, then you are Abraham's seed, and heirs according to the promise" (Gal. 3:28-29 NKJV).

When Jesus was preparing to leave the earth after His resurrection, He instructed His disciples to minister to the *whole world.* "Jesus came and told his disciples, 'I have been given all authority in heaven and on earth. Therefore, go and make disciples of *all the nations*, baptizing them in the name of the Father and the Son and the Holy Spirit. Teach these new disciples to obey all the commands I have given you. And be sure of this: I am with you always, even to the end of the age" (Matt. 28:18-20 NLT, emphasis added). When the Messiah comes again, He will be the same Messiah for all. Arguments and rhetoric between Christians and Jews will stop. The Jews are the "apple of God's eye" (Deut. 32:10), but the Christians are also the apple of God's eye because they have been grafted into that apple tree.

The New Testament recognizes that those Jews characterized as "true Jews" have realized that Jesus is the Messiah (see Rom. 9–11). They accept that Jesus was the Son of God, did miracles, performed healings, raised people from the dead, was Himself raised from the dead, and forgave sins. They believe that Jesus described Himself as the fulfillment of the law and the prophets of the Jewish Scriptures. They also acknowledge that to enter heaven they must believe on or trust in Yeshua Hamaschiach, the Jewish Messiah, Jesus Christ, as shown by obedience to His commands.

Muhammad's message to the world was very different. He described himself as a prophet who had come to present the true picture of Allah to mankind. He claimed no power to forgive sins, required people to follow the five pillars of Islam (which he made up), and said that a person's destiny depended on Allah's determination of his or her good and bad deeds as they related to those five pillars. Here is a quick comparison of some of the other major differences between Christ and Muhammad:

Jesus of Christianity	Muhammad of Islam
Jesus claimed to be one with the God of Abraham, Isaac, and Jacob.	Muhammad claimed to be the greatest prophet of the moon god.
Jesus said that eternal life could be obtained by believing in Him and receiving God's forgiveness.	Muhammad said that eternal life could only be guaranteed by participating in *jihad*.
Jesus died for the lost sheep.	Muhammad killed the lost sheep.
Jesus did miracles.	Muhammad did none.
Jesus could cast out demons.	Muhammad could not.
Jesus treated women with respect.	Muhammad treated women as chattel or property.
Jesus was sinless.	Muhammad was not.
Jesus said that it was possible to have a personal relationship with the God of the Bible.	Muhammad said that a personal relationship with Allah was not possible.

It is interesting to note that moderate Muslims, traditional Catholics, orthodox Christians, and Christians by birth or association are all able to live together in relative peace. They subscribe to a system of justification before God by works, and none of them take their religion seriously *on a personal and relational basis*. However, while they may all be at peace outwardly, those following true Islam count them among their enemies, who must be converted or exterminated. Pray that the truth of the God of Abraham, Isaac, and Jacob will be obvious to Muslims *and* to all Christians and Jews.

FOR STUDY AND REFLECTION

Consider the following questions based on the material you read in this chapter:

1. The Koran and Hadith present a different picture of Christ from the one found in the New Testament. Based on the information from this chapter, make a list of ten characteristics of the Jesus of the Bible and ten characteristics of the Jesus of Islam.

	Jesus of Christianity	Jesus of Islam
1.		
2.		
3.		
4.		
5.		
6.		
7.		
8.		
9.		
10.		

2. What is the difference between the Muslim view of forgiveness and the Christian view of forgiveness?

3. What is the one way Muslims can be sure of forgiveness and of a place in their idea of paradise?

4. What evidence do Muslims cite to support their claim that Jesus also said that believers would go to paradise if they took part in *jihad*? What was Jesus actually saying? In what ways did Christ tell His disciples to make a difference in the world?

5. According to Islam and their holy books, what happens to a Black Muslim who dies in *jihad* and stands before Allah for judgment? What evidence do we find that Black Muslims are treated differently by the Muslims in the countries of the Middle East?

6. In what ways is the gospel of Jesus different from the message that Muhammad proclaimed? In what ways is Christianity an "inclusive gospel"?

Now, watch the next ten minutes of *Jihad in America*. Play the video from the speech by Sheik Abdul Wali Zindani to just after the section where the children are singing a *jihad* chant at a summer camp in the Midwest. After watching the video, consider the following questions:

1. How do you feel about the meetings and rallies being held in the United States?

2. What do you think of the analogy about shouting "fire" in a crowded movie theater as it applies to the fundamental Muslims?

3. Do you find it surprising that the United States has granted tax-exempt status to organizations that have used the funds raised to support terrorism? Why or why not?

4. Does this part of the video raise other questions for you?

CHAPTER EIGHT

THE CONCEPT OF LOVE IN ISLAM

IN HER BOOK, *Not Without My Daughter,* author Betty Mahmoody tells the story of how she met and fell in love with a Muslim doctor practicing in the United States. The couple had an adorable daughter, and for a while all seemed to be going well. Then in 1984, her husband told Betty that they would be taking a two-week trip to Tehran to visit family. Betty was reluctant to go, but she ultimately acquiesced to her husband's wishes and made the trip.

When Betty and her daughter arrived in Iran, they immediately experienced culture shock. They were no longer free to do what they wanted or even dress as they pleased. Both Betty's husband and the Islamic society in which they found themselves now dictated their every move. Betty wanted to leave, but her husband informed her that they would not be returning to the United States.

Betty went to the U.S. Embassy, where she was told that even though she had the legal right to leave the country, she could not do so with her daughter. In Iran, the father has legal custody of his children. So Betty returned to her husband's home, which she now had to share with his relatives. There, her husband's relatives mistreated her by beating her and locking her inside her room for days. She was also forced to witness her daughter being scolded and punished at the school she was required to attend.

What is amazing about this story is that these similar misfortunes happen to thousands of young women from non-Islamic cultures each year. White slavery is alive and well in more places than we can imagine. Given this and all of the other atrocities we hear are being committed in Muslim countries, one can only wonder at the statement that is often made in the media that Islam is a *religion of love.* In this chapter, we will look at the evidence from the Koran and from the practices that exist in Muslim countries today to see if this claim has any merit.

MUSLIM TEACHINGS ON LOVING OTHERS

If Islam were truly a religion of love, one would expect the concept to be mentioned numerous times in the Koran, Islam's most holy book. The Koran does mention love, but nowhere are the practitioners of Islam required to show it to others. Instead, the text focuses more on the uncertain and changing conditions under which Allah might choose to grant his love. As Avi Lipkin, former editor and translator for the news department under Israeli Prime Minister Yitzhak Shamir, states, "When you find the word love, it is said that Allah loves this and Allah loves that."

However, it doesn't appear that Allah loves all that much, because the word appears only twenty-four times in the entire Koran. Compare this to the number of times it appears in the Tanakh and the New Testament: 11,571. For every time you read the word "love" in the Koran, it appears 482 times in the Bible. This textual evidence does not seem to support the idea that Islam is all that concerned about the way people show love to one another.

In truth, the Koran actually promotes hostility between different groups of people. In Sura 5:51 we read, "Believers, take neither Jews nor Christians to be your friends; they are friends with one another. Whoever of you seeks their friendship shall become one of their number and God does not guide [those Jewish and Christian] wrongdoers." Sura 5:57 adds the following: "Say, People of the Book [Jews and Christians], is it not that you hate us [Muslims] only because we believe in Allah and in what has been revealed to others, and because most of you are evildoers?"

The Koran states that Muslims should have nothing to do with Christians and Jews. It claims that these individuals are evildoers—despite the fact that Muslims claim God and Allah to be the same, and that Jesus was Allah's messenger to bring the gospel to the world. Time and again, we hear stories of Muslims persecuting those who follow Christ, as the following news stories relate:

- In Jordan, Samer and Abeer, a couple who had converted to Christ, were arrested and detained by the country's security police. At the hearing, Samer was asked to "alter his confession," or recant his Christian faith. An Islamic judge told him, "You cannot be a Christian, you must come back to Islam." When Samer refused, he was convicted of apostasy. The courts forfeited his inheritance, declared his marriage illegal, and took away custody of his son.[1]
- In Pakistan, Muslim extremists, with the help of the country's police, set fire to a Christian man who refused to convert to Islam. Previously, religious leaders had told the man to convert back to Islam with his entire family or face "dire consequences." The man's wife was raped by the local police as the couple's three children were forced to watch.[2]
- In Egypt, Coptic Christians, who number between eight and fifteen million in the country, have become wary of legal loopholes used to acquit Muslims who carry out attacks against Christians. Those who become Christians are subjected to harassment by the State Security Investigation, which often arrests converts for "insulting" Islam or "threatening national security."[3]
- In Iran, state police arrested and tortured a newly converted Christian couple for holding Bible studies and attending a house church. After the couple was released, authorities warned them that if they returned to their house church or had contact with other Christians, they would lose custody of their daughter and be punished under Islamic law.[4]

We find a completely different message in the Judeo-Christian Scriptures. In Deuteronomy 6:4-5, Moses told the Israelites, "Hear, O Israel! The Lord is our God, the Lord is one! You shall love the Lord your God with all your heart and with all your soul and with all your might" (NASB). In Leviticus 19:18, God commanded His people, "Never seek revenge or bear a grudge against anyone, but love your neighbor as yourself. I am the Lord" (NLT).

Jesus Christ Himself said that out of the 613 commandments given in the Old Testament, these two were the most important. We see this when one of the teachers of the law approached Jesus and asked Him to identify the greatest command. Jesus answered by giving him two: "The most important commandment is this: 'Hear, O Israel! The Lord our God is the one and only Lord. And you must love the Lord your God with all your heart, all your soul, all your mind, and all your strength.' The second is equally important: 'Love your neighbor as yourself.' No other commandment is greater than these" (Mark 12:29-31 NLT).

Jesus also had a different teaching from Muhammad on how His followers were to treat one another—and those who did not necessarily share their same faith. He told His listeners, "I say, love your enemies! Pray for those who persecute you! In that way, you will be acting as true children of your Father in heaven. . . . If you love only those who love you, what good is that? Even corrupt tax collectors do that much. If you are kind only to your friends, how are you different from anyone else? Even pagans do that" (Matt. 5:44-47). This is a true message of love and compassion, and one that we do not find in Islam.

MUSLIM TEACHINGS ON WOMEN

As we have discussed in previous chapters, women have never been very welcome in the Islamic religion, and they are not treated as equals today in Muslim society. In fact, women are generally viewed as property to be used as males see fit and are given few—if any—rights. Based on what we find in the Koran, it is apparent that Muhammad sanctioned this hierarchy between men and women.

In Sura 4:34 we read, "Men have authority over women because God has made the one superior to the other, and because they spend their wealth to maintain them. Good women are obedient. They guard their unseen parts because God has guarded them. As for those from whom you fear disobedience, admonish them and send them to their beds apart and beat them." This is why Muslim women wear *chadors* (the long black robes with hoods and slits for eyes) and why Muslim men are allowed to beat their wives.

There are other restrictions on women as well. According to Sura 33:53, a woman is not allowed to answer the door if her husband is not home—even if it is her brother or another relative. Sura 33:33 states that a woman must stay in her home and cannot travel without the permission of her father or husband. Sura 4:34 states that a woman cannot refuse to have sexual relations with her husband. If she does, it is permissible for the husband to beat her into submission or kill her in the process. In Iran, it is illegal for a woman to die a virgin. In that country, they have rape squads of men who are assigned to make sure that no woman violates this law.

Current information from Islamic countries reveals that women are sometimes used as tools to gain new converts to Islam. Often, these attempts focus on visiting male medical doctors and other professionals who are working in the Muslim nation. A typical scenario is that the professional will have Muslim women on his staff, and by prearrangement with fundamentalist Muslims, one of these women will sexually attack him when she is alone with him. After a short while, a group of armed Muslims will burst into the room and demand an explanation. They will give the man the choice of marrying the girl and becoming a Muslim or dying immediately. Most of these professionals decide to convert to Islam (at least until they can try to escape).

Just how poorly women are viewed in Islam can be seen by the place they are given in the afterlife. As previously noted, if a man dies in *jihad*, he gets to go directly to heaven and is given the stamina to enjoy sex with seven virgins in each of seven mansions. It is not clear from the Koran what the reward is for a woman who dies in *jihad*, but to encourage female bomb murderers, Muslims now claim that a woman who dies in such a way gets to spend a night with Muhammad. What a treat!

Many Islamic scholars believe that hell is primarily comprised of women. According to a Hadith by Sahih of al-Bukari:

Muhammad said, "I saw Paradise and I stretched my hand to pluck a bunch of grapes, then I saw Hell (fire), and I have never before seen such a horrible sight as that the majority of its dwellers were women." The people asked, "O Allah's apostle, what is the reason for that?" He replied, "Because of their ungrateful-ness." It was said, "Do they believe in Allah?" He replied, "They are not thankful to their husbands and they are ungrateful for the favors done to them. Even if you do some good to one of them all your life when she sees some harshness from you she will say, 'I have never seen any good from you.'"

Dr. Joseph Abd El Schafi, in his book *Behind the Veil,* sums up the plight of women in Muslim countries: "How miserable women are in Muhammad's view! He orders men *to scourge* them, forces young women to *marry against their will,* and *exploits single women* as tools of pleasure. He also declares that most *people in hell are women.*"[5]

Again, we find a completely different view in the Judeo-Christian Scriptures. In the Bible, there are 6,370 references to the word "wife," and 4,722 of these references occur in the Old Testament. This tells us that the relationship between husbands and wives is an important topic in the sacred writings of the Jews and Christians. One passage that especially illuminates the way in which husbands and wives are commanded to treat one another is found in Paul's letter to the Ephesians:

> Submit yourselves to one another because of your reverence for Christ. Wives, submit to your husbands as to the Lord. . . . Husbands, love your wives just as Christ loved the church and gave his life for it. . . . Men ought to love their wives just as they love their own bodies. A man who loves his wife loves himself. . . . As the scripture says, "For this reason a man will leave his father and mother and unite with his wife, and the two will become one." There is a deep secret truth revealed in this scripture, which I understand as applying to Christ and the church. But it also applies to you: every husband must love his wife as himself, and every wife must respect her husband.
> —Eph. 5:21-23, 25-28, 31-33 GNT

In the Judeo-Christian Scriptures, God commands His followers to treat one another with love and respect—and this includes the relationship between men and women. The same is not true in Islam, which gives men free rein to act as they desire against women and even goes so far as to claim that women are the main occupants of hell.

THE POISON OF HATE

Avi Lipkin has accurately stated that when people hate, they prepare a vial of poison for those they detest and then drink the vial. This is an excellent summary of what happens to a Muslim (or anyone else for that matter) from a psychological, emotional, and physiological stance when that person spotlights his or her hateful thoughts on someone else. First, that person begins to turn away from positive and helpful things in life and focuses only on the negative. This powerful negative emotion interferes with the person's thinking and his or her ability to enjoy life.

Because the body is an integrated organism, this affects the individual's brain. It causes it to secrete stress-related hormones that ultimately result in physical damage to the person's body. At the same time, the person's brain suppresses the release of good hormones that enable him or her to enjoy life to the fullest. In a spiritual sense, when a person hates another individual, that person is only harming himself or herself and is destroying his or her spiritual life in the process. The hate often has no effect on the person at whom it is directed—in fact, the other person might not even realize that the other individual feels so strongly about him or her.

Indeed, it is possible to prepare a vial of poison for those we hate and then drink that vial. No matter how we slice it, hate is a powerful, unhealthy, and negative emotion. Jesus gave us a better way to deal with our enemies. While we are to hate evil and bring justice to the world, we are not to hate the people themselves.

In Islam, you can steal, lie, kill, burn, pillage, cheat, and rape if it is done for a "just" cause. This means that a person can do just about anything if he or she defines that action as being just. This is the ultimate expression of relativism, in that anything a person wants to do is deemed acceptable and good because the person has elevated himself to the position of an authority that can make such a decision. In Islam, it is truly "anything goes." This is completely opposite of the divine and incontrovertible truth that operates in the universe.

The Judeo-Christian God is the God of love, the Bible is a book of love, and the Messiah is a Messiah of love. The same cannot be said of the god of Islam.

Muhammad spoke of a master and slave relationship with Allah. He never spoke of loving Allah, and he never spoke of loving other Muslims. His religion was a system of laws and regulations, and he controlled his followers with rewards and punishments.

Pray and thank God for revealing His love to us through the Scriptures and the Messiah. Pray that others, including Muslims, might experience that same love in their lives and experience freedom and fulfillment.

Angry Muslims in England

Islam Will Dominate the World (from England)

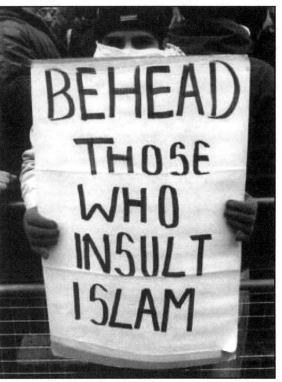

Behead Those Who Insult Islam

Butcher Those Who Insult Islam (from England)

Exterminate Those Who Slander Islam

Anti Freedom (in England)

Europe's 911 on the Way (from England)

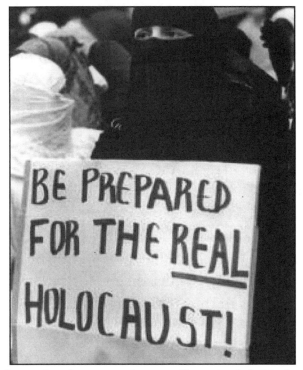

The Real Holocaust is Coming (from English Muslims)

FOR STUDY AND REFLECTION

Many in the media claim Islam is a religion of love. However, based on what we read in the Koran and the stories we hear of intolerance in many Muslim nations today, this claim tends to ring hollow.

Consider what you have learned in this chapter as you answer the following questions:

1. How does God say we should interact with one another based on the information we find in the Old Testament and the New Testament?

2. What was Muhammad's view on loving others? What were his views on how Allah showed love? How does the Koran say Muslims should behave toward those who are not Muslims?

3. Having read this chapter, as a woman would you be tempted to go to an Islamic country to marry a rich sheik or a prince? Why or why not?

4. If a man dies in *jihad*, he goes to heaven and is given the energy to enjoy sex with seven virgins in each of seven mansions. What happens if a woman dies in *jihad*? Does she get to be one of the virgins?

5. How do parents feel when their children are abusing and fighting one another? How do they feel when they ignore and disrespect them? Does this bear any likeness to the relationship between God and man? Why or why not?

Now watch the next ten minutes of *Jihad in America*. Play the video from just after the children at the summer camp to the interview with Professor Sami Al-Arian. After watching the video, answer the following questions:

1. What was Sheik Mohammad Al-Asi's response when Steve Emerson asked him at what time the United States would become a war front? According to Al-Asi, will the United States ever become a war front in the minds of Islamists?

2. What is the ICP? How does the organization describe itself? What group does it support? What is the purpose of the ICP?

3. What else have you learned in the media about Professor Sami Al-Arian?

4. Do you think he had connections to terrorist groups? Why or why not?

CHAPTER NINE

THE CONCEPT OF PEACE IN ISLAM

ONE WEEK AFTER September 11, 2011, President George W. Bush held a press conference to denounce the terrorists who had carried out the attacks against the World Trade Center and the Pentagon. He stated that Muslim leaders of nations around the world had been appalled at the events they saw unfolding on their television screens, and that these acts of violence violated the fundamental tenets of the Islamic faith. The president stated that Islam is fundamentally *a religion of peace,* and that billions of people worldwide find comfort, solace, and *peace* in the religion.[1]

To support his view, the president cited Sura 30:10: "In the long run evil in the extreme will be the End of those who do evil; for that they rejected the Signs of Allah, and held them up to ridicule" (Sura 30:10). What is interesting about the context of this verse is that it appears in what is known as the "Sura of the Romans," a passage that calls Muslims to look forward to the victory it prophesies of the Emperor Heraclius' Christians over the Persian Zoroastrians.[2] This is not exactly a message of peace. Nor are these passages that we find in the Koran:

Let not the unbelievers think they will ever get away. They have not the power to do so. Muster against them all the men and cavalry at your command, so that you may strike terror into the enemy of Allah and your enemy. Muhammad-Prophet, rouse the faithful to arms. If they (the non-Muslims) incline to peace (and accept Islam) make peace with them.

—Sura 8:59

Fight and slay the infidels wherever ye find them, and seize them, beleaguer them, and lie in wait for them in every stratagem of war.

—Sura 9:5

Make war on unbelievers and hypocrites, and deal rigorously with them.

—Sura 9:73

Who are the infidels, hypocrites, and unbelievers Muhammad is describing in these verses? Obviously, they are those who do not subscribe to the religion of Islam. Muhammad describes how these non-believers are to be treated: seized, fought, slain, and made war against. Their punishment is execution, dismemberment, or—at the very least—exile. Muhammad states that Muslims must muster against these individuals to "strike terror" into the enemy of Allah. Muhammad's strong wording in these passages provides us with insight into just how upset he was at the Jews and Christians, the ones he called "the People of the Book," when they refused to follow him and pay his taxes. Another passage in the Koran that echoes these sentiments is found in Sura 8:12-16:

I shall cast terror into the hearts of the infidels. Strike off their heads, strike off the very tips of their fingers! That was because they defied Allah and his apostle, Mohammad. He that defies Allah and his apostle Mohammad shall be sternly punished by Allah. We said to them: "Taste this. The scourge of the Fire awaits the unbelievers." Believers [Muslims], when you encounter the infidels on the march, do not turn your backs to them in flight. If anyone on that day turns his back on them, except for tactical reasons, or to join another band, he shall incur the wrath of Allah, and hell shall be his home; an evil fate.

In an article in *The London Times,* Hassan Butt, a former jihadist, states, "Only when Muslims admit that 9/11 and 7/7 [a London bombing] were the work of Muslim terrorists can we move forward to the next juncture: which is recognizing the hard truth that Islam does permit the use of violence. Muslims who deny this, preferring instead to mouth easy platitudes about how Islam is nothing but a religion of peace, make the job easier for the radicals who can point to passages in the Koran, set down in black and white, that instruct on the killing of unbelievers."[3]

In this chapter, we will look at some examples of this and explore the idea that Islam is a religion of peace.

THE APES AND THE SWINE

In Sura 5:60, Muhammad penned these words: "Shall I tell you who will receive a worse reward from Allah? Those whom God has cursed and with whom he has been angry, transforming them into apes and swine and those who serve the devil. Worse is the plight of these and they have strayed farther from the right path." Who are the apes and swine that serve the devil?

Yasser Arafat, the man whose atrocities we discussed at the beginning of this book, is credited with writing a nursery rhyme that is taught to young children in every Muslim country. The gist of the rhyme is to "kill the Children of the Apes on Saturday" and to "kill the Children of the Swine on Sunday." Every Muslim schoolchild knows that the Children of the Apes are the Jews (who worship on Saturday) and the Children of the Swine are the Christians (who worship on Sunday). Such indoctrination allows young Muslims to grow up viewing Jews and Christians as apes and swine, which makes it much easier to kill them.

This view is further dramatized by a ridiculous story found in the Hadith. According to this story, when Jesus was a little boy, He went out to play. When He got outside, He could not find the other children anywhere, so He went to their parents' houses and asked where they had gone. The parents, not wanting their children to play with Jesus, lied to Him and said that the children were away. In fact, the parents were keeping them inside to keep them away from the influence of Jesus. When the young Jesus found out about this, He cursed these children and turned the Jewish children into monkeys and the Gentile children into pigs.

When we examine stories such as these found in the holy writings of Islam, we can only come to the conclusion that Muslims are of two types: Revolutionary Muslims and Evolutionary Muslims. Revolutionary Muslims study Islam, understand what it says, and have no difficulty carrying out its commands by participating in violent *jihad*. We might refer to these groups as "fundamentalists" or "radicals." Evolutionary Muslims also accept all of Islam, but they prefer to let others do the fighting, while they work toward the gradual transformation of societies. Ironically, it is the "radicals" who seem to be the ones who are practicing Islam in accordance with their holy writings.

Islam doesn't want those who refuse to follow the tenets of Islam merely imprisoned or ignored. It wants them *dead*. As Sura 8:67 states, "It is not for a Prophet that he should have prisoners of war (and then free them only with ransom) until he had made a great slaughter (among his enemies) in the land." This does not speak well to the claim that Islam is a religion of peace.

THE KORAN IN ACTION

One of the favorite verses of some of the fundamentalist Muslims in Algeria is Sura 5:33: "Their punishment is execution or crucifixion, of the cutting of hands and feet from the opposite sides, or exile from the land." The fundamentalist groups in this African nation apply this verse vigorously and literally against other Muslim groups it deems not radical enough in their theology. In particular, these groups target Muslims who collaborate with the more moderate Muslim government.

Once these fundamentalist Muslims identify a village where they feel the people are not truly faithful to Allah (as they interpret it), they enact an eight-step plan. First, they wait until the men of the village go out at five o'clock or six o'clock in the morning to work in the fields. Next, the fundamentalist Muslims surround the village and demand that the women prepare a festive meal for them. The men eat the meal and take hallucinatory drugs, and then they rape the women and slit their throats. Next, they kill the children and the old men whom they have forced to watch the rape, torture, and murder of their mothers, sisters, and daughters. Finally, they cut the arms and legs off the bodies with chainsaws and mutilate them.

They leave the bodies in the open so when the men come home in the evening, they can see what happens to those who are not faithful enough to Allah.

As hard as it is may be to comprehend, this story details Muslims treating other Muslims in a fashion that is consistent with their holy book, the Koran. In the same way that Yasser Arafat ordered his followers to commit atrocities against other Muslims whom he deemed not faithful to Islam, these groups read the Koran at face value and strike out against those they consider infidels. One would be hard pressed to say that the Muslim groups they attack are finding "comfort and solace and *peace* in the religion."

Since I first researched this story, a revival has taken place in Algeria. A seminary in Cairo, Egypt, began sending teams of Arab Christians into Algeria. As a result, many Muslims (more than 26,000 at last count) have come to believe in Jesus Christ. These former Muslims are risking their lives by trusting in the God of Abraham, Isaac, and Jacob. This is astounding in such a closed culture.

ISLAM AND DEMOCRACY

Certainly, these actions are carried out by what we would consider to be radical Islamists. In the story above, for instance, these groups struck out against the more moderate Muslims, who collaborated with the Algerian government. This raises an interesting question: Is it possible for a true democracy and peace to exist and prosper in more moderate Islamic regimes?

The answer appears to be no. In fact, democracy in Islamic countries bears little resemblance to the form of "government by the people and for the people" that we see in Western nations. In the "democracy" of Egypt, for example, it is illegal for more than three people to meet in public without the government's permission. In many other Islamic "democracies," 99 percent of the votes are cast for the incumbent. The people know that the other one percent will not be around for the next election.

We would also do well to note that none of this has changed in light of the various more recent "democracy movements" in the Middle East. Indeed, the movement in Egypt is replacing the sham democracy referred to in the previous paragraph with one that is much more repressive. They have just started to organize the "modesty police" in order to subjugate women in the same way they are treated in other more extreme Islamic countries like Iran. Likewise, the overall thrust in the various countries involved is to replace a problematic but nonetheless somewhat slightly moderate Islamic leadership with a group that is much more faithful to the teachings of the Koran as understood by those considered to be extremists, such as the Muslim Brotherhood.

An interesting tidbit to digest in light of these "pro-democracy" movements is that in many cases they are seemingly being fomented by people from outside the country in question. For example, in Egypt, Christian missionaries on the ground reported through e-mails to those who care about them in the United States that the protestors were not local. They seemed to be of the same racial group as the residents of the country, but they spoke a completely different Arabic dialect that was not immediately identifiable. Interestingly, these particular protestors also reportedly all had the same make and model of cell phone with which they were in communication with their compatriots. Clearly, more was at work here than reported on the evening news.

King Fahd of Saudi Arabia, a member of the Saud family monarchy that has ruled the country since 1932, once said, "The democratic system that is predominant in the world is not a suitable system for the peoples of our region. The system of free elections is not suitable to our country." Christian Snouck Hurgronje, a Dutch scholar on Middle Eastern culture, also noted that "Islam has never favored democratic tendencies." Samuel P. Huntington, an American political scientist, suggested that "Western ideas of individualism, liberalism, constitutionalism, human rights, equality, liberty, and the rule of law, democracy, free markets, the separation of church and state often have little resonance in Islamic, Confucian, Japanese, Hindu, Buddhist, or Orthodox cultures."[4]

Perhaps the reason why democracy does not work in these nations can be summed up by this statement from Mawlana Abul Ala Mawdudi, the founder of Pakistan's fundamentalist movement: "Islam is not a normal religion like the other religions in the world, and Muslim nations are not like normal nations. Muslim nations are very special because they have a command from Allah to rule the entire world and to be over every nation of the world."

Mawlana notes that Islam is a revolutionary faith that comes to destroy "any government made by man." The goal of Islam is to rule the entire world and force those who do not practice Islam to convert to the faith. In this respect, Islam doesn't care about the people on the land or who owns the land—if those people are not Muslims, they are to be destroyed. Islam is to fight any nation or power in the world that tries to get in the way of that one singular goal, and it can use any option at its disposal to bring about that worldwide revolution. Furthermore, Mawlana believes Islam is a political system that must replace all other forms of government. "Islam is not just a spiritual religion," he states. "Islam is a way of life. It is a heavenly system revealed to our world through the angel Gabriel, and the responsibility of Muslims is to destroy any other system in the world and to replace it with the Islamic system."

From this, we see that the only way a true democracy can survive in these nations is by discarding the tenets of Islam and adopting those of the Judeo-Christian Scriptures. This is because of the basic differences between the values of Islam and those of Judaism and Christianity. In the words of Ravi Zacharias, "America functions within a moral framework, and that framework can be meaningful only when attached to a Creator." This is the reason why George Washington in his farewell address warned his country not to attempt to build a moral framework apart from God:

> Of all the disputations and habits that lead to political prosperity, religion and morality are indispensable supports. In vain would that man claim the tribute of patriotism who should labor to subvert these great pillars of human happiness. . . . These finest props of duties of men and citizens. . . . And let us with caution indulge the supposition that morality can be maintained without religion. Whatever may be conceded to the influence of refined education on the minds of peculiar structure, reason and experience both forbid us to expect that national morality can prevail in exclusion of religious principle.

Let's not fool ourselves: it is historically accurate to say that the religious principles about which George Washington spoke are those emanating from trusting in the God of Abraham, Isaac, and Jacob, and the Messiah. In fact, the closing paragraph of the Declaration of Independence states, "We, therefore, the Representatives of the United States of America, in General Congress *assembled, appealing to the Supreme Judge of the world . . . and for the support of this declaration, with a firm reliance on the protection of Divine providence,* we mutually pledge to each other our lives, our fortunes, and our sacred honor" (emphasis mine).

Sacredness of life and the protection of God are woven into the fabric of our national existence. It is upon this foundation that the principles of democracy in this country were established. Democracy cannot exist in Muslim nations because the foundation of those cultures operates on a system that seeks to annihilate any form of government other than Islamic government. Once again, we see that such a system does not support the notion that Islam is a religion of peace.

TARGET: AMERICA

The first Islamic terrorist strike with a plane against a building of national importance in a Western nation occurred in December 1994. A group known as the Algierian Groupe Islamique Armie hijacked an Air France jetliner with the intent of crashing it into the Eiffel Tower. Most of the members of this group had been trained by American Special Forces during the war in Afghanistan against the Soviet Union.

However, the attempt failed because once the terrorists commandeered the plane, they realized they didn't know how to fly it. The Air France pilots refused to follow their orders to fly the plane into their target. Eventually, the plane landed in Marseilles, where it was stormed by French police.

The terrorists learned from their mistake. Several years later, Islamic groups sent pilots to seventeen different flight schools in America to train as commercial pilots. On September 11, 2001, these pilots successfully hijacked three planes and flew them into the World Trade Center and the Pentagon. A fourth plane that many believe was planned to crash into the Capitol Building went down in Pennsylvania.

After the attacks, Americans discovered that the United States had become a target for these Islamic terrorist organizations. But why? One of the reasons is because to Muslims, America represents "the People of the Book," or Jews and

Christians. America supports Israel, whom even moderate Islamic nations do not believe has the right to exist. As James Dobson, formerly of Focus on the Family, has stated, "As long as we are pledged to defend Israel and its 'covenant land,' we will be targeted by Muslim terrorists."[5] America also supports Christianity around the world. More Christian missionaries come from the United States than from any other country, and this represents a threat to the spread of Islam. In addition, America is a "government of the people, by the people, and for the people," which makes it heathen to Muslim thinking because Allah is to be the head of all government.

To Muslims, America is the source of all they consider evil: pornography, alcohol, homosexual rights, evil music, evil fashion, and evil culture. Mark Galli, managing editor of *Christianity Today,* noted that Islamic militants are angry at the West for exporting "hedonism and materialism into their very homes through television, enticing Muslims to become lazy and morally corrupt." Galli quoted a 1985 communication from the terrorist group Hezbollah: "Our way is one of radical combat against depravity, and America is the original root of depravity."[6]

Charles Colson, a Christian leader and cultural commentator, stated, "America's increasing decadence is giving aid and comfort to the enemy. When we tolerate trash on television, permit pornography to invade our homes via the Internet, and allow babies to be killed at the point of birth, we are inflaming radical Islam. . . . When radical Islamists see American women abusing Muslim men, as they did in the Abu Ghraib prison, and when they see news coverage of same-sex couples being 'married' in U.S. towns, we make our kind of freedom abhorrent—the kind they see as a blot on Allah's creation."[7] For Christians in this nation, this should serve as a wake-up call. The lessons of history reveal that we in the church must be diligent in engaging these moral battles.

THE TRUE GOSPEL OF PEACE

In the end, we see that Islam is in no way a message of peace. The true gospel of peace can only be found in the message of Christ: "Peace is what I leave with you; it is my own peace that I give you. I do not give it as the world does. Do not be worried and upset; do not be afraid" (John 14:27).

Throughout the New Testament, we find instructions on how we are to live and be at peace with one another. The author of Hebrews states, "Try to be at peace with everyone, and try to live a holy life, because no one will see the Lord without it" (Heb. 12:14 GNT). The apostle writes, "Turn away from evil and do good. Work hard at living in peace with others" (1 Peter 3:11 NLT). In Philippians 4:7, Paul says, "If you do this, you will experience God's peace, which is far more wonderful than the human mind can understand. His peace will guard your hearts and minds as you live in Christ Jesus" (NLT). In 2 Timothy 2:22, he adds, "Pursue faith and love and peace, and enjoy the companionship of those who call on the Lord with pure hearts" (NLT).

This is the inner peace of mind and spirit that Christ desires us to have. While we will encounter many trials and sorrows in this life, we know that we can take heart because Christ has overcome the world (see John 16:33), and He has promised to never leave or forsake us (see Heb. 13:5). This is a peace that Islam does not offer. "Fighting is obligatory for you, much as you dislike it. But you may hate a thing although it is good for you and love a thing although it is bad for you" (Sura 2:216).

As we conclude this book, take a moment to think about the Muslims living in Asia, Africa, the Middle East, Europe, Southeast Asia, and the rest of the world, who are not experiencing the peace found in Christ. These individuals have been deceived and need to have their eyes, minds, and hearts opened to the truth. Most demographers agree that of the 184 countries in the world at the time of this writing, seventy could be considered Islamic. When you consider the number of followers of Islam in many of these nations, you realize just how many individuals are living on the edge of darkness:

Afghanistan: 31,100,000
Albania: 3,600,523
Algeria: 33,333,216
Azerbaijan: 8,120,247
Bahrain: 698,585
Bangladesh: 150,448,339

Brunei: 374,577
Bosnia and Herzegovina: 3,964,000
Burkina Faso: 13,228,000
Chad: 9,885,661
Comoros: 711,417
Côte D'Ivoire: 3,310,520

Djibouti: 496,394
Egypt: 80,335,036
England: 60,776,238
Ethiopia: 75,100,000
France: 64,057,790
Indonesia: 234,693,997
Iran: 65,397,521
Iraq: 27,499,638
Jordan: 6,053,193
Kazakhstan: 15,284,929
Kuwait: 1,500,000
Lebanon: 3,925,502
Libya: 5,700,000
Malaysia: 24,821,286
Mali: 11,925,402
Morocco: 33,757,175
Niger: 12,894,865

Nigeria: 133,530,000
Oman: 2,567,000
Pakistan: 164,741,924
Qatar: 907,229
Saudi Arabia: 23,000,000
Senegal: 12,521,581
Sierra Leone: 6,144,562
Somalia: 9,890,000
Sudan: 39,379,58
Syria: 19,000,000
Tajikistan: 7,076,598
Tunisia: 10,276,158
Turkey: 71,158,647
United Arab Emirates: 4,496,000
Uzbekistan: 28,300,000
Yemen: 22,230,531
Zanzibar: 800,000

Approximate total: 1,546,600,000

This number is so large that the human mind cannot easily comprehend it. To put these numbers in perspective, imagine that you have $1,546,600,000. If you lived a thousand years and spent a million dollars per year, earning only .5 percent (one-half of one percent interest) per year after taxes, you would still have $199,845,145,812 left over to leave to your heirs. That is more than one hundred times the amount you had when you started!

A FINAL CHALLENGE

You now know more about the truth behind Islam than most teachers, administrators, professors, pastors, politicians, counselors, lawyers, doctors, financial professionals, bankers, and business people. It is my hope that you will now be better equipped to do battle in the cultural war against the forces of Islam. Being so equipped, I want to direct your attention to a few quotes from people in our history who did their part to win this war on behalf of the God of Abraham, Isaac, and Jacob. Let's first examine this statement from Samuel Adams, often called the father of the American Revolution:

> If you prefer wealth to liberty and the tranquility of servitude rather than the animated contest of freedom, then go home in peace. We seek neither your council nor your arms. But bow down and lick the hands that feed you. May your chains rest lightly upon you. And may posterity forget that you were our countrymen.

Teddy Roosevelt, one of our greatest presidents, noted, "Far better it is to dare mighty things, to win glorious triumphs, even though checkered by failure, than to take rank with those poor spirits who neither enjoy much nor suffer much because they live in the gray twilight that knows not victory nor defeat." In another speech, Roosevelt made these observations:

> It is not the critic who counts, not the man who points out how the strong man stumbled, or where the doer of deeds could have done them better. The credit belongs to the man who is actually in the arena; whose face is marred by dust and sweat and blood; who strives valiantly; who errs and comes short again and again; who knows the great enthusiasms, the great devotions, and spends himself in a worthy cause; who, at the best knows in the end the triumph of high achievement; and who, at worst, if he fails, at least fails while daring greatly, so that his place shall never be with those cold and timid souls who know neither victory nor defeat.

Patrick Henry, one of our nation's Founding Fathers, said, "We are apt to shut our eyes against the painful truth, and listen to the song of that siren until she transforms us into beasts. Is this the part of wise men engaged in the great and arduous struggle for liberty? Are we disposed to be the number of those who having eyes see not, and having ears hear not, the things that so nearly concern our temporal salvation? For my part, whatever anguish of spirit it may cost, I am willing to know the whole truth, to know the worst, and to provide for it."

As you close this book and reflect on everything we have covered, I ask you to consider this final reminder from the apostle Paul about winning the cultural war:

> A final word: Be strong with the Lord's mighty power. Put on all of God's armor so that you will be able to stand firm against all strategies and tricks of the Devil. For we are not fighting against people made of flesh and blood, but against the evil rulers and authorities of the unseen world, against those mighty powers of darkness who rule this world, and against wicked spirits in the heavenly realms. Use every piece of God's armor to resist the enemy in the time of evil, so that after the battle you will still be standing firm. Stand your ground. . . . Pray at all times and on every occasion in the power of the Holy Spirit. Stay alert and be persistent in your prayers for all Christians everywhere.
>
> —Eph. 6:10-14, 18 NLT

Pray that each of us will put on the armor of God and do our part to win the cultural war in which we are all engaged. Pray also that nonbelievers from all cultures will come to experience the freedom and joy of life that is available through the Messiah and a relationship with Him. Finally, pray that the United States will be faithful to its founding vision and underlying faith and for the freedom of all of those who have been enslaved by Islam.

FOR STUDY AND REFLECTION

Contrary to what many people in politics and the media have claimed, Islam is *not* a religion of peace, and billions of people worldwide have *not* found comfort, solace, and peace in it. As you consider the information in this chapter, make a list of what the following Bible passages say about the concept of peace:

Scripture	What it says about peace
John 14:27	
Philippians 4:7	
2 Timothy 2:22	
Hebrews 12:14	
1 Peter 3:11	

1. Does the peace that you read about in these passages mean that believers will have an easy life or never have to fight? How would you explain this?

2. George Bush said, "Islam is a religion of peace." Why do you think he said that?

3. Whom does the Koran consider to be infidels, hypocrites, and unbelievers? How does Allah direct his followers to deal with these individuals?

4. Who are the Apes and the Swine? Why are these groups referred to in this way?

5. How do the quotes from Samuel Adams, Teddy Roosevelt, and Patrick Henry relate to our position in the cultural war that is now taking place in our country and in the world at large?

Now watch the last section of *Jihad in America*. Play the video from after the interview with Professor Sami Al-Arian to the end. After watching the video, answer the following questions:

1. What do you think about the statement, "It is easier to come to the United States as a terrorist than a refugee"?

2. Why do radical Muslims call the United States "the Great Satan"?

3. Why do those of us in Western society have trouble understanding the fundamentalist Islamic mindset? Why is there "no democracy in Islam"?

4. What is the daily problem faced by moderate Muslims? Who is the most threatened by the militant Muslims?

5. How are the moderate Muslims similar to moderate Christians and Jews? Do moderate Muslims understand their religion, or is it just a part of the culture to them?

TWELVE COMMANDMENTS FOR SHARING THE GOSPEL WITH MUSLIMS

(LARGELY FROM DR. MARK A. GABRIEL)

THE FOLLOWING ARE twelve commandments to keep in mind when you are sharing the gospel with Muslims. Much of this information comes from a former Muslim, who has significant insight into the Islamic mindset. After reading this book on Islam, you should be able to understand why each of these points is important.

1. *Use the Word of God.* Muslims respect the sacred books: the law of Moses, the book of Psalms, the gospels, the rest of the Bible, and the Koran. Let the Word of God speak for itself. The gospels are the best portions with which to start, particularly Matthew and Luke.
2. *Be constantly in prayer*. It is the Holy Spirit who wins people to Christ. Seek His guidance and power as you present the Word.
3. *Be a genuine friend*. Saying, "Hello, how are you?" isn't enough. If you really care, show it by inviting Muslims into your home, sharing your time with them, and helping them with their problems.
4. *Ask thought-provoking questions*. Help Muslims reach their own conclusions about the gospel. Good questions to ask are, "Do you have assurance that God will accept you?" "What does the Koran teach about forgiveness?"

"May I show you what the Bible teaches?" These questions show that you have an interest in the important things of life.

5. *Listen attentively*. When you ask a question, courtesy requires that you listen to the answer no matter how long it takes. You will be surprised at how much you will learn.

6. ***Present your beliefs openly***. State what you believe clearly and without apology, showing Scripture passages that support your statements. In this way, you can place the responsibility for doctrine where it belongs: on the Word of God. Talk about sin and how it affects people's lives. Describe how sin is the biggest problem in our world today, and share how Jesus forgives sins. Most Muslims recognize that they are living in sin, but they don't know how to get forgiveness. This is paradoxical for them, as it flies in the face of the teachings of Islam and reveals innate characteristics of human nature and conscience.

7. ***Reason; don't argue***. Arguing may win the point but lose the battle. There are some points on which you can argue forever without achieving a thing—except closing a mind against you.

8. ***Never denigrate Muhammad or the Koran***. This is as offensive to them as speaking disrespectfully about Christ or the Bible is to us.

9. ***Respect their customs and sensitivities***. Don't offend Muslims by putting your Bible (a holy book) on the floor, speaking too freely about sex (Muslims consider it dirty), appearing too familiar in casual relationships with the opposite sex, refusing hospitality, making jokes about sacred topics (such as fasting, prayer, or God), or offering them pork or alcohol. Women are more acceptable to practicing Muslims if they wear a long dress as opposed to pants or shorts.

10. ***Do not concentrate on the cross***. The cross is a direct contradiction to the lies they have been taught. If they come around, it will then become meaningful to them.

11. ***Live a life consistent with the Judeo-Christian Scriptures***. Your life must show the results of putting the teachings of the Tanakh and the New

Testament documents into practice. Without this and the evidence of a personal relationship with the Messiah, all other efforts are for nothing.

12. ***Persevere***. Muslims have a lot of rethinking to do when they are confronted with the gospel, but rest assured that the Word of God will do its work in His good time. Above all, be humble. Speak with love. This will make a way for you.

FURTHER NOTES

Remember that it is a death sentence for a Muslim to take a Jew or a Christian for a friend. "Those who reject Islam must be killed. If they turn back from Islam, take hold of them and kill them wherever you find them" (Sura 4:89).

For this reason, if a Muslim says he is your friend, he is either lying to Allah or lying to you. If he is lying to Allah, you should love that person and pray for him, realizing that he may be open to the gospel. If the person is lying to *you*, you should still love him and pray for him, but don't turn your back on that person.

The World Council of Churches has embraced Islam. The Pope has gone to Damascus and kissed the Koran in the mosque. Most conservative Christian scholars say it is heresy to support Islam in any way, because it delegitimizes Judaism and Christianity. Misinformed Jews or Christians who dialogue with terrorists are thus legitimizing the religion that delegitimizes them.

Love the Muslim, but be wary of Islam. Do not despise them, but fear the implications of their occultic religion.

ENDNOTES

Chapter 1: The Great Islamic Conspiracy

1. Steven Emerson, *Terrorists Among Us: Jihad in America,* Ventura Distribution, November 13, 2001.
2. "Jihad," Wikipedia.com. http://en.wikipedia.org/wiki/Jihad#cite_ref-0.
3. "Yasser Arafat," Wikipedia.com. http://en.wikipedia.org/wiki/Yasser_Arafat.
4. From a statement made by General Ariel Sharon: "Arafat was the man who ordered the bellies of pregnant Arab women slit open while their husbands looked on; he was the man who ordered the hands of Arab children cut off while their parents watched in horror. Arafat was the man who ordered innocent Arab brothers in Nablus to be hung by their chins on butcher hooks until they were dead, and personally slit open the stomachs of pregnant Israeli women and murdered children." http://www.healingontheweb.org/prophecy/invade01.htm.
5. Ibid.
6. Jeff Jacoby, "The Dead Children Have Been Forgotten," *The Boston Globe,* January 2005.
7. Statement by General Ariel Sharon. http://www.healingontheweb.org/prophecy/invade01.htm.

8. "Munich Massacre," Wikipedia.org. http://en.wikipedia.org/wiki/Munich_massacre.

9. "Yasir Arafat's Timeline of Terror," Middle East Issues, Committee for Accuracy in Middle East Reporting in America, November 13, 2004. http://www.camera.org/index.asp?x_article=795&x_context=7.

10. Jeff Jacoby, "The Dead Children Have Been Forgotten," *The Boston Globe*, January 2005.

11. Yii-Ann Christine Chen, "Why Do People Say Muslim Now Instead of Moslem?" George Mason University's History News Network, January 21, 2002. http://hnn.us/articles/524.html.

12. For information on unreached people groups, visit the Joshua Project website at www.joshuaproject.net.

13. Don Richardson, quoted in Stuart Robinson, *Mosques and Miracles* (Australia: City Harvest Publications, 2003), p. 1.

14. "How Many Muslims Are There in the U.S. and the Rest of the World?" ReligiousTolerance.org, data from the Council on American-Islamic Relations. http://www.religioustolerance.org/isl_numb.htm.

15. Samuel P. Huntington, *The Clash of Civilizations and the Remaking of World Order* (New York: Touchstone, 1996).

16. "Muslims More Numerous than Catholics: Vatican," Reuters, March 30, 2008. http://uk.reuters.com/article/2008/03/30/uk-vatican-muslims-idUKL3068682420080330.

17. Dr. Khalid Al-Mansour, *The Challenges of Spreading Islam in America and Other Essays* (San Francisco: First African Arabian Press, 1980).

18. "Zero Population Growth," Wikipedia.org. http://en.wikipedia.org/wiki/Zero_population_growth.

19. Ed Vitagliand, *Europe's Chastisement: How the Abandonment of Christianity May Be Leading to Disaster* (Agape Press, 2006).

20. Kathy Shaidle, "The Coming Islamic Takeover of Russia," ZLM, March 2009.

21. Walter Rademacher, quoted in Gudrun Schultz, "German Population Plunge 'Irreversible,' Federal Stats Office Admist," Life Site News, November 9, 2006. http://www.lifesitenews.com/news/archive/ldn/2006/nov/06110903.

22. Muammar Al-Gaddafi, speech broadcast on Al-Jazeera TV (Qatar), April 10, 2006.

Chapter 2: The Cultural War

1. "Religion in the United States," Wikipedia.org. http://en.wikipedia.org/wiki/Religion_in_the_United_States.

2. These estimates of the Muslim population in North America are from Israeli intelligence, which today is the best source for these types of statistics.

3. Diana Eck, *A New Religious America: How a "Christian Country" Has Become the World's Most Religiously Diverse Nation* (San Francisco, HarperCollins, 2002).

4. "The Global Muslim Population: Projections for 2010–2013," The Pew Forum on Religion and Public Life, January 27, 2011. http://pewforum.org/future-of-the-global-muslim-population-regional-americas.aspx.

5. "Dearborn, Michigan," Wikipedia.org. http://en.wikipedia.org/wiki/Dearborn,_Michigan.

6. Omar Khalidi, "Mosques in the United States of America and Canada," U.S. Embassy Germany. www.pbs.org/weta/crossroads/.../mosque/MosquesofNorthAmerica.pdf.

7. "Islam in the United States," Wikipedia.org. http://en.wikipedia.org/wiki/Islam_in_the_United_States. Allison Keyes, "A History of Black Muslims in America," NPR, February 7, 2011. http://www.npr.org/templates/story/story.php?storyId=4811402.

8. As of June 2002, the total number of individual incarcerated was 2,019,234, of which 818,900 were African-American males. "The African-American Males: A Distressing Rap Sheet National Data," February 24, 2005. http://diverseeducation.com/article/4372/.

9. In this war, we are all at the front in some way, whether we realize it or not.

10. "Brigitte Bardot," Wikipedia.org. http://en.wikipedia.org/wiki/Brigitte_Bardot#Politics_and_legal_issues.

11. Emily Belz, "Wilders' Side," *World,* November 7, 2009.

12. Amnon Rubenstein, "A New Era of Brutality," Zola Levitt Ministries, January 2005.

13. "Our Partners in Peace," Zola Levitt Ministries, May 2005.

14. "Schoolboys Punished with Detention for Refusing to Kneel in Class and Pray to Allah," *Daily Mail,* July 4, 2008. http://www.dailymail.co.uk/news/article-1031784/Schoolboys-punished-detention-refusing-kneel-pray-Allah.html.

15. "Homeland Insecurity: Quantico Mosque Leader Promoted," WorldNetDaily, December 14, 2006. http://www.wnd.com/?pageId=39297.

16. Omar Ahmad, from an interview with the *San Ramon Valley Herald* in 1998, quoted in Nonie Darwish, *Now They Call Me Infidel* (New York: Penguin Books, 2006).

17. "Fethullah Gülen's Missionary Schools in Central Asia and their Role in the Spreading of Turkism and Islam," *Religion, State and Society,* vol. 31, no. 2, 2003.

18. "Objectives of Charter Schools with Turkish Ties Questioned," *USA Today.* http://www.usatoday.com/news/education/2010-08-17-turkishfinal17_CV_N.htm.

19. Ibid.

20. Many of these nations, including Russia and Uzbekistan, have now outlawed the establishment of FGC schools. Even in the Netherlands—a country that promotes tolerance at all costs—the government has cut funding to FGC schools because of their aggressive promotion of Islam. In the United States, the Terek ibn Zayed Academy in Minnesota was deemed so radically Islamic that the Minnesota Department of Education issued two citations against it.

21. "Fethullah Gülen's Grand Ambition," *The Middle East Quarterly,* Winter 2009. http://www.meforum.org/2045/fethullah-gulens-grand-ambition#ftn51.

22. Material in this section adapted from Steve Elwart, "Islam Taught in Charter Schools: The Gülen Movement," *Personal Update: The News Journal of Koinonia House,* vol. 21, no. 2, February 2011, pp. 7-13.

23. "Islamic Saudi Academy," Wikipedia.org. http://en.wikipedia.org/wiki/Islamic_Saudi_Academy.

Chapter 3: The Strange Origins of Islam

1. There at least thirteen different ways to "correctly" spell Muhammad's name. Note that Muhammad was illiterate, so he wouldn't have been able to spell it himself.

2. "Adolf Hitler," Wikipedia.org. http://en.wikipedia.org/wiki/Adolf_Hitler#Rebuilding_of_the_party.

3. Some sources claim this number is considerably understated.

4. Patrick Cox, "Can Islam Reform?" Zola Levitt Ministries, September 2008.

5. William Welty, PhD, "Thomas Jefferson's Koran." http://www.khouse.org/articles/2007/691/print.

6. "Armenian Genocide," Wikipedia.org. http://en.wikipedia.org/wiki/Armenian_Genocide.

7. Ruth Lapioth and Moshe Hirsh, *The Jerusalem Question and its Resolution: Selected Documents* (Dordrecht, The Netherlands: Martinus Nijhoff Publishers, 1994).

8. Ibid.

Chapter 4: Tenets and Customs of Islam

1. Don Richardson, *Secrets of the Koran* (Ventura, CA: Regal, 2008), p. 38.

2. "Hajj," Wikipedia.org. http://en.wikipedia.org/wiki/Hajj.

3. Quoted in Edwin Arnold, *Poetical Works of Edwin Arnold* (New York: John B. Alden Publisher, 1883), p. 201.

4. "Affront to Justice: Death Penalty in Saudi Arabia," Amnesty International, 2008. www.amnesty.org/en/library/asset/.../mde230272008en.pdf.

Chapter 5: The Koran and the Bible

1. Caravans are mentioned numerous times throughout Scripture, the oldest and most reliable documents we have on the subject. See Genesis 37:25; Judges 5:6, 8:11; 1 Kings 10:2; 2 Chronicles 9:1; Job 6:18-19; Isaiah 21:13, 60:6; Ezekiel 27:25; Luke 2:44.
2. Jalal al Din 'Abdul Rahman b. Abi Bakr al Suyuti, *al-Itqan fi 'ulum al-Qur'an,* cited in John Burton, *Collection of the Qur'an* (New York: Cambridge University Press, 1977), p. 117.
3. Abū Muḥammad 'Alī ibn Aḥmad ibn Sa'īd ibn Ḥhazm was an eleventh-century Sunni Islamic scholar who produced a reported four hundred works, of which only forty still survive.

Chapter 6: Allah and the God of the Jewish and Christian Scriptures

1. *Sahih Muslim,* collected by Imam Muslim, book 17, no. 4206.
2. Karen Armstrong, *Jerusalem: One City, Three Faiths* (New York: Ballantine Books, 1997), p. 221.

Chapter 7: Jesus of Islam and Jesus of the Bible

1. Samuel G. Miller, "Jesus of the Koran," July 2005, p. 5.
2. Ibid.
3. Robert Hughes, "The Fraying of America," *Time,* February 3, 1992.
4. "2004 Indian Ocean Earthquake and Tsunami," Wikipedia.org, http://en.wikipedia.org/wiki/2004_Indian_Ocean_earthquake_and_tsunami; "ACEH: Conflict and Reconciliation: Indonesia Facts," Cultural Survival, 2000, http://www.culturalsurvival.org/publications/cultural-survival-quarterly/indonesia/aceh-conflict-reconciliation.
5. Seah Chiang Nee, "Tsunami: A Disappointing Muslim Response," Blessed Quietness.com. http://blessedquietness.com/alhaj/stingymuslimsnations.htm.

Chapter 8: The Concept of Love in Islam

1. Mindy Belz, "Apostasy Rules," *World,* April 9, 2005.

2. Fareed Khan, "Wife Raped for Their Christian Faith," Zola Levitt Ministries, June 2010.

3. Jerry Dykstra, "Egypt: Free to Attack Christians," *Today's Christian,* May/June 2007, p. 53.

4. "Human Race," *World,* July 12/19, 2008, p. 13.

5. Dr. Joseph Abd El Schafi, *Behind the Veil* (Longwood, FL: Xulon Press, 2008). It is disturbing to note that since publishing this book, Dr. Schafi has disappeared from sight. Has he simply gone underground, or has he met with a worse fate?

Chapter 9: The Concept of Peace in Islam

1. President George W. Bush, address given at the Islamic Center of Washington, D.C., delivered September 17, 2001. http://www.americanrhetoric.com/speeches/gwbush911islamispeace.htm.

2. "Surat al-Rum," Wikipedia.org. http://en.wikipedia.org/wiki/Ar-Rum.

3. Hassan Butt, "Muslim Heads Stuck Firmly in the Sand," *The Times,* July 14, 2007. http://www.timesonline.co.uk/tol/comment/columnists/guest_contributors/article2072587.ece.

4. Samuel P. Huntington, *The Clash of Civilizations* (New York: Simon and Schuster, 1998).

5. James Dobson, "Family News from Dr. James Dobson," Focus on the Family, October 2006.

6. Mark Galli, citied in Charles Colson, "The Moral Home Front," *Christianity Today,* October 2004.

7. Ibid.

SOURCES

Books, Audio Books, and Periodicals

Abrams, Israel. *Campaigns in Palestine from Alexander the Great.* London: Argonaut Publishers, 1922.

Al-Huda Islamic Center, Inc. *Beginners Guide to Performing Islamic Prayers.* Al-Huda Islamic Center, Athens: GA.

Al-Mansour, Dr. Khalid. *The Challenges of Spreading Islam in America and Other Essays.* San Francisco: First African Arabian Press, 1980.

Ali, Muhammad. *The Muslim Prayer Book.* Dublin, OH: Ahmadiyya Anjuman Ishaat, 1992.

Ashraf, Sh. Muhammad. *Salat or Islam Prayer Book.* Bensenville, IL: Lushena Books. 2002.

Bard, Mitchell G. *Myths and Facts: A Guide to the Arab-Israeli Conflict.* Chevy Chase, MD: American Israeli Cooperative Enterprise, 2001.

Bawer, Bruce. *While Europe Slept: How Radical Islam Is Destroying the West from Within.* New York: Doubleday, 2006.

Bearman, P.J. *Encyclopedia of Islam.* Boston, MA: Brill Academic Publishers, 2005.

Berlinski, Claire. *Menace in Europe: Why the Continent's Crisis Is America's, Too.* New York: Three Rivers Press, 2007.

Blair, Sheila S. and Jonathan M. Bloom. *The Art and Architecture of Islam.* New Haven, CT: Yale University Press, 1996.

Blomberg, Craig L. *The Historical Reliability of the Gospels.* Downers Grove, IL: Inter-Varsity Press, 1987.

Bloom, Allan. *The Closing of the American Mind.* New York: Simon and Schuster, 1988.

Bork, Robert H. *Slouching Toward Gomorrah: Modern Liberalism and American Decline.* New York: HarperCollins, 1996.

Bruce, F.F. *The New Testament Documents: Are They Reliable?* Downers Grove, IL: InterVarsity Press, 1981.

Caner, Ergun Mehmet and Emir Fethi Caner. *More Than a Prophet: An Insider's Response to Muslim Beliefs About Jesus and Christianity.* Grand Rapids, MI: Kregel Publications, 2003.

Caner, Ergun Mehmet and Emir Fethi Caner. *Unveiling Islam: An Insider's Look at Muslim Life and Beliefs.* Grand Rapids, MI: Kregel Publications, 2002.

Cleveland, William L. *History of the Modern Middle East.* Boulder, CO: Westview Press, 2000.

Corse, Jerome R. PhD. *Atomic Iran.* Nashville, TN: WND Books, 2005.

Coulter, Ann. *How to Talk to a Liberal (If You Must).* New York: Crown Forum, 2004.

Darwish, Nonie. *Now They Call Me Infidel: Why I Renounced Jihad for America, Israel and the War on Terror.* New York: Sentinel Books, 2006. (Darwish is a the daughter of a Muslim *shahid*.)

El Schafi, Dr. Abd. *Behind the Veil: Unmasking Islam.* Mumbai, India: Pioneer Book Company, 2002. (This is an excellent resource produced by a scholar from the Middle East and is not, at the time of this writing, available in most book stores.)

Emerson, Steven. *American Jihad: The Terrorists Living Among Us.* New York: Free Press, 2003. (An excellent book.)

Evans, Michael D. *Beyond Iraq: The Next Move.* Lakeland, FL: White Stone Books, 2003.

Evans, Michael D. *The American Prophecies.* Nashville, TN: Warner Faith, 2004.

Folger, Janet L. *The Criminalization of Christianity.* Sisters, OR: Multnomah Books, 2005.

Formenton, Fabio. *Oriental Rugs and Carpets.* England: Littlehampton Book Services, Ltd., 1972.

Friedman, Dr. David. *Sudden Terror: Exposing Militant Islam's War Against the United States and Israel.* Clarksville, MD: Messianic Jewish Resources International, 2002.

Gabriel, Bridgette. *Because They Hate: A Survivor of Islamic Terror Warns America.* New York: St. Martin's Press, 2006.

Gabriel, Bridgette. *They Must Be Stopped: Why We Must Defeat Radical Islam and How We Can Do It.* New York: St. Martin's Press, 2008.

Gabriel, Dr. Mark A. *Islam and Terrorism.* Lake Mary, FL: Strang Communications, 2002. (Dr. Gabriel is a former professor of Islamic history at Al Azhar University in Cairo. He was imprisoned and tortured for becoming a believer in Jesus Christ.)

Gabriel, Dr. Mark A. *Islam and the Jews: The Unfinished Battle.* Lake Mary, FL: Strang Communications, 2003.

Gabriel, Dr. Mark A. *Jesus and Muhammad.* Lake Mary, FL: Strang Communications, 2004. (Very interesting book by former Muslim.)

Gilbert, Martin. *The Rutledge Atlas of the Arab Israeli Conflict.* New York: Routledge Press, 2008.

Hart, George. *The Routledge Dictionary of Egyptian Gods and Goddesses.* New York: Routledge Press, 2005.

Hitchcock, Mark. *The Coming Islamic Invasion of Israel.* Sisters, OR: Multnomah Books, 2006.

Horowitz, David. *Unholy Alliance: Radical Islam and the American Left.* Washington, D.C.: Regnery Publishing, Inc., 2004.

Hunt, Dave. *Israel, Islam, and the Last Days* (audio book). Winnipeg, CA: Winnipeg Prophecy Conference, 2003.

Hunt, Dave. *Judgment Day: Islam, Israel and the Nations.* Bend, OR: The Berean Call, 2005.

Huntington, Samuel P. *The Clash of Civilizations and the Remaking of World Order.* New York: Touchstone, 1996.

Hurley, Victor. *Jungle Patrol: The Story of the Philippine Constabulary.* Boston, MA: E.P. Dutton, 1938.

Ice, Thomas. *Why the World Hates Israel* (audio book). Coeur d'Alene, ID: Compass International, Inc.

Irwin, David K. *What Christians Need to Know About Muslims.* Springfield, MO: Center for Ministry to Muslims, 1983.

Khalidi, Omar. "Import, Adapt, Innovate: Mosque Design in the United States." Houston, TX: *Saudi Aramco World,* November/December 2001.

Kingsriter, Del. *Questions Muslims Ask That Need to be Answered.* Springfield, MO: Center for Ministry to Muslims, 2001.

Kingsriter, Del. *Sharing Your Faith with Muslims.* Springfield, MO: Center for Ministry to Muslims, 1986.

Klein, Aaron. *Schmoozing with Terrorists.* Los Angeles, CA: WND Books, 2007.

Kohen, Rabbi Manachem. *Prophecies for the Era of Muslim Terror: A Torah Perspective on World Events.* New York: Lambda Publishers, Inc. 2007.

The Koran (alternate spelling *Qur'an*). New York: Penguin Books, 2006.

Laqueur, Walter. *The Last Days of Europe: Epitaph for an Old Continent.* New York: Thomas Dunne Books, 2007.

Le Baron Bowen, Richard Jr., Frank P. Albright, et al. *Archaeological Discoveries in South Arabia.* Baltimore, MD: Johns Hopkins Press, 1958.

Levitt, Zola. *The Trouble with Christians; The Trouble with Jews.* Dallas, TX: Zola Levitt Ministries, 1996.

Limbaugh, David. *Persecution: How Liberals Are Waging War Against Christianity.* Washington, D.C.: Regnery Publishing Inc., 2003.

Lindsey, Hal. *The Everlasting Hatred: The Roots of Jihad.* Lake Elsinore, CA: Oracle House Publishing, 2002.

Lipkin, Avi. *Shiite/Sunni: The Two Houses of Islam.* Coeur d'Alene, ID: Koinonia House, 2007.

Lipkin, Avi. *Sleeping in America.* Coeur d'Alene, ID: Koinonia House, 2003.

Lipkin, Avi. *The New Crusades.* Coeur d'Alene, ID: Koinonia House, 2004.

Maalouf, Tony. *Arabs in the Shadow of Israel.* Grand Rapids, MI: Kregel Publications, 2003. (Note: This book is written by a closet Muslim who has an agenda of misleading the uninformed.)

Mahmoody, Betty. *Not Without My Daughter.* New York: St. Martin's Press, 1987.

Maududi, Syed Abul A'la. *Jihad in Islam.* Translated by Abdul Waheed Kan. Pakistan: Islamic Publications, Ltd.

McTernan, John P. *As America Has Done to Israel.* New Kensington, PA: Whitaker House, 2006.

Meagher, Paul Kevin, Thomas C. O'Brien and Consuelo Maria Aherne, eds. *Encyclopedia of Religion.* Washington, D.C.: Corpus Publishers, 1979.

Middleton, Andrew. *Rugs and Carpets.* England: Mitchell Beazley, 1997.

Miller, William M. *A Christian's Response to Islam.* Phillipsburg, NJ: P&R Publishing, 1976.

Milton, Giles. *White Gold: The Extraordinary Story of Thomas Pellow and Islam's One Million White Slaves.* New York: Farrar, Straus and Giroux, 2004.

Missler, Dr. Charles. *Footprints of the Messiah* (audio book). Coeur d'Alene, ID: Koinonia House, 1992.

Missler, Dr. Charles. *Muslims: Who Are They and What Do They Really Want?* (audio book). Coeur d'Alene, ID: Compass International, Inc.

Missler, Dr. Charles. *Roots of War* (audio book). Coeur d'Alene, ID: Koinonia House, 2002.

Missler, Dr. Charles and Avi Lipkin. *A Legacy of Hate* (audio book). Coeur d'Alene, ID: Koinonia House, 2000.

Montgomery, John Warwick. *God's Inerrant Word.* Minneapolis, MN: Bethany House Publishers, 1974.

Mordecai, Victor. *Is Fanatic Islam a Global Threat.* Talmidim Publishing, 2003.

Mordecai, Victor. *Islamic Threat Updates.* Almanac No. 1, #5762. Talmidim Publishing, 2003.

Morey, Robert. *Islamic Invasion.* Eugene, OR: Harvest House Publishers, 1992.

Netanyahu, Benjamin. *A Durable Peace: Israel and Its Place Among the Nations.* New York: Warner Books, 1993.

Peck, Ron. *The Shadow of the Crescent: The Growth of Islam in the U.S.* Springfield, MO: Center for Ministry to Muslims, 2001.

Peter, Joan. *From Time Immemorial: The Origin of the Arab-Jewish Conflict Over Palestine.* Chicago: JKAP Publications, 2001.

Phillips, Melanie. *Londonistan.* New York: Encounter Books, 2006.

Phillips, Wendell. *Qataban and Sheba: Exploring Ancient Kingdoms on the Biblical Spice Routes of Arabia.* London: Victor Gollancz Ltd., 1955.

Posten, Larry and Carl F. Ellis, Jr. *The Changing Face of Islam in America.* Camp Hill, PA: Horizon Books, 2000.

Price, Randall. *Fast Facts on the Middle East Conflict.* Eugene, OR: Harvest House Publishers, 2003.

Rafiqul-Haqq, M. and P. Newton. *The Place of Women in Pure Islam.* Mumbai, India: Pioneer Book Company, 1992.

Rollins, James. *Sandstorm.* New York: HarperCollins, 2004.

"Sheba." *The Columbia Electronic Encyclopedia,* sixth edition. New York: Columbia University Press.

Steyn, Mark. *America Alone.* Washington, D.C.: Regnery Publishing Inc., 2006. (This is an excellent resource on Islam and demographics)

Spencer, Robert. *Islam Unveiled: Disturbing Questions About the World's Fastest Growing Faith.* New York: Encounter Books, 2002.

Spencer, Robert. *Onward Muslim Soldiers: How Jihad Still Threatens America and the West.* Washington, D.C.: Regnery Publishing Inc., 2003.

Spencer, Robert. *The Complete Infidel's Guide to the Koran.* Washington, D.C.: Regnery Publishing Inc., 2009.

Spencer, Robert. *The Myth of Islamic Tolerance: How Islamic Law Treats Non-Muslims.* New York: Prometheus Books, 2005.

Spencer, Robert. *The Politically Incorrect Guide to Islam.* Washington, D.C.: Regnery Publishing Inc., 2005.

Sperry, Paul. *Infiltration: How Muslim Spies Have Penetrated Washington.* Nashville, TN: Thomas Nelson, 2005.

Stoner, Peter. *Science Speaks.* Chicago, IL: Moody Press, 1958.

Timmerman, Kenneth R. *Preachers of Hate: Islam and the War on America.* New York: Three Rivers Press, 2004.

Trifkovic, Serge. *The Sword of the Prophet: Islam, History, Theology, Impact on the World.* Salisbury, MA: Regina Orthodox Press, 2007.

Walvoord, John F. *Armageddon, Oil and Terror: What the Bible Says About the Future of America, the Middle East, and the End of Western Civilization.* Carol Stream, IL: Tyndale, 2007.

Warraq, Ibn. *Why I Am Not a Muslim.* Amherst, NY: Prometheus Books, 2003.

Water, Mark. *World Religions Made Simple.* Chattanooga, TN: Living Ink Books, 2002.

Williams, Paul L. *The Day of Islam: The Annihilation of America and the Western World.* New York: Prometheus Books, 2007.

Woolman, David S. "Fighting Islam's Fierce Moro Warriors—America's First War with Suicidal Islamic Warriors." Leesburg, VA: *Military History Magazine,* 2002. (Woolman is a Manila-based author living in the Philippines.)

Ye'or, Bat. *Eurabia: The Euro-Arab Axis.* Madison, NJ: Fairleigh Dickson University Press, 2005.

Youssef, Michael. *America, Oil and the Islamic Mind.* Grand Rapids, MI: Zondervan, 1991.

Zacharias, Ravi. *Jesus Among Other Gods: The Absolute Claims of the Christian Message.* Nashville, TN: W Publishing Group, 2002.

Zacharias, Ravi. *Light in the Shadow of Jihad: The Struggle for Truth.* Sisters, OR: Multnomah Books, 2002.

Videos and DVDs

Emerson, Steven. *Jihad in America.* Public Broadcasting Service. Arlington, Virginia. (This video was made in 1994 with the help of the FBI, the CIA, and the U.S. State Department. It was buried for being anti-Muslim, but it was not—it was anti-terrorism. The producer was blacklisted and put under an Islamic death sentence.)

The Jesus Film Project. Campus Crusade for Christ International. Orlando, FL. www.jesusfilm.org. (Designed to be helpful to Muslims.)

Lipkin, Avi. *Five Deceptions of Islam.* http://www.youtube.com/view_play_list?p=FA0B59C816E4F4C8.

Missler, Dr. Charles. *Israel, Muslims and the Last Days.* http://www.youtube.com/watch?v=P5jmV7-VEXc.

Missler, Dr. Charles. *Jihad: America's New War.* Coeur d'Alene, ID: Koinonia House, 1992.

More than Dreams: The Amazing Phenomenon of Jesus' Appearing to Muslims in Dreams. Damascus Films. www.familychristianmovies.com.

Websites and Online Resources

Boykin, Keith. *The Racial Index of 2004.* www.keithboykin.com.

Campus Crusade for Christ International. Orlando, FL. www.ccci.org.

Center for Ministry to Muslims. Springfield, MO. www.cmmequip.org.

Central Intelligence Agency (CIA). *The World Factbook.* Washington, D.C., 2010. www.cia.gov.

Levitt Newsletter. Zola Levitt Ministries. May 2005. http://www.levitt.com/levletter.html.

Mattar, Dr. Mohamed. The Protection Project. Johns Hopkins University School of Advanced International Studies. www.protectionproject.org.

Microsoft Corporation. *Microsoft Encarta Multimedia Encyclopedia.* Redmond, WA: Microsoft Corporation, 1993-2009. www.microsoft.com.

Middle East Outreach. www.MiddleEastOutreach.org.

The Islam Project. www.islamproject.org. (An organization devoted to propagandizing the American education system with misinformation.)

Islamic Legal Forum of the American University Washington College of Law. www.wcl.american.edu/org.

Shamoun, Sam. "Abraham and the Child of Sacrifice—Isaac or Ishmael?" Answering Islam: A Christian-Muslim Dialogue. http://www.answering-islam. org/Shamoun/sacrifice.htm.

U.S. Department of Justice, Bureau of Justice Statistics. *Database on the United States Prison Population.* Washington, D.C., 2009. http://bjs.ojp.usdoj.gov.

Windows to the Universe. University Corporation for Atmospheric Research (UCAR), The Regents of the University of Michigan, 1995-2000. www. windows.ucar.edu.

Woll, Johanna. *Islamic Architecture, Art and Urbanism.* MIT Libraries: Islamic Architecture. http://libguides.mit.edu/islam-arch.

World Magazine. January 15, 2005 edition. Asheville, NC. www.worldmag. com.

WinePressPublishing
Great Books, Defined.

To order additional copies of this book call:
1-877-421-READ (7323)
or please visit our website at
www.WinePressbooks.com

If you enjoyed this quality custom-published book,
drop by our website for more books and information.

www.winepresspublishing.com
"Your partner in custom publishing."